Financing African Economies from Within

Chief Economists of Government

CEoG
CHIEF ECONOMISTS OF
GOVERNMENT NETWORK

This book is a product of the Chief Economists of Government (CEoG) network. CEoG is a peer network of chief economic advisors to heads of states in Sub-Saharan Africa, with the goal of promoting evidence-based policymaking in the region. The network is convened by the World Bank's Africa Chief Economist Office. However, the findings, interpretations, and conclusions expressed herein do not necessarily reflect the views of the World Bank, nor the Executive Directors they represent. This publication was made possible with the financial support of the Think Africa Partnership.

Contents

List of Figures

List of Tables

List of Boxes

Acknowledgments

This book is the first authored by members of the Chief Economists of Government (CEoG) program, a network comprising over 40 chief economic advisors to heads of state or government across sub-Saharan Africa. The book aims to gather lessons and experiences from African chief economists on domestic financing, which will be critical for the continent's future. Additionally, it supports one of the CEoG program's key objectives, peer learning, while assisting countries in mobilizing greater internal revenue for development.

The coordination and preparation of the book were led by Mohamed Lamine Doumbouya, Mamadou Tanou Balde and Maximilien Onga Nana. The chapters were authored by Abdallah Msa, Amina Rwakunda, Elung Paul Che, Gnounka Diouf, Marcellin Bilomba, Mohamed Lamine Doumbouya, Momodou Dibba, Sen Narrainen, Stephane Ouedraogo, and Trudi Makhaya, in collaboration with Colette Nyirakamana, George Marbuah, Maimouna Diakité, and Nara Monkam.

The team extends its gratitude to Albert Zeufack, former Chief Economist for the Africa Region, who initiated this effort, and to his successor, Chief Economist for the Africa Region, Andrew Dabalen. This appreciation extends to the Chief Economist team, as well as the CEoG Secretariat, for their support. This secretariat includes James Cust, Justice Mensah, Maximilien Onga Nana, Mamadou Tanou Balde, Juliette Lehner, Hannah Grupp, Olumide Lawal, Abrah Desiree Brahima, and Constantine Manda.

The team is also grateful for the insightful comments received from participants of the CEoG annual forums and external reviewers Anand Rajaram and Franz Krige Siebrits.

Lastly, the team acknowledges funding support from the Think Africa Partnership (TAP) Trust Fund.

About the Contributing Economic Advisors of Heads of State or Government

Marcellin Bilomba

From March 2019 to 2022, Mr. Marcellin Bilomba served as Principal Advisor to the DRC President Félix Tshisekedi at the Economic College before being appointed Managing Director at Sonahydroc. Prior to this, he held several key positions: Managing Director of Transkin International S.a.r.l in Geneva from January 1998 to June 2000 and in Kinshasa from 2006 to 2019; Managing Director of B&M Services SARL in Paris from February 2004 to November 2005; and Managing Director of Geneva Business Institute from June 2000 to October 2003.

Elung Paul Che

Mr. Elung Paul Che is the Deputy Secretary General at the Presidency of Cameroon and has held several administrative positions in the country. Formerly the General Manager of the Hydrocarbon Prices Stabilization Fund (CSPH), he was appointed Minister Delegate in the Ministry of Finance. He has also served in the following positions: Paymaster General in the Northwest and Southwest Regions, Director of Treasury, Director General of Treasury, Auditor at the Bank of Central African States (BEAC), Commissioner at the Central African Banking Commission (COBAC), Commissioner at the Financial Markets Commission of BEAC, member of the Audit Committee of the BEAC, and focal point of the reform of the Central African Economic and Monetary Community's (CEMAC) payment system, among others.

Momodou K. Dibba

Mr. Momodou K. Dibba served as the Director of Policy Analysis in the Department of Strategic Policy and Delivery, Office of the President of Gambia. This role was preceded by a five-year stint at the Ministry of Finance and Economic Affairs. In 2022, he also served as the National Coordinator of the National Social Protection

Secretariat, Office of the Vice President. He worked on the National Social Protection Act 2024, which established the National Social Protection Agency and introduced the first legislation on social assistance in the country. In January 2025, he was appointed as the first Executive Director of the Agency. Before his appointment, Mr. Dibba worked as a Development Economics Expert for Somaliland on their National Development Plan III during a year-long sabbatical from the civil service. Mr. Dibba holds an MSc in Economics from the University of Berne, Switzerland, and is currently a PhD candidate in Economics at the University of Witwatersrand, Johannesburg, South Africa.

Gnounka Touré Diouf

Mrs. Gnounka Touré Diouf served as Minister and Chief Economic Advisor in charge of Economic Affairs to the former President of Senegal, Macky Sall. In this role, she oversaw economic policy, including the Plan Sénégal Emergent. She has also served as a Member of the Monetary Policy Committee at the Central Bank and monitored integration policy with the African Union, New Partnership for Africa's Development (NEPAD), and West African Economic and Monetary Union (WAEMU). Mrs. Diouf is the G20 Sherpa for Senegal and has been involved in the Compact with Africa implementation. Previously, she was Deputy Secretary General of the Ministry of the Economy and Finance, where she designed various economic policy strategies, including Senegal's Accelerated Growth Strategy. She holds a master's degree from the Ecole Nationale d 'Administration (ENA) in Senegal and graduated from the Institute for Economic Development at the University of Pittsburgh. She is invited as a CEoG Expert.

Mohamed L. Doumbouya

Dr. Mohamed Doumbouya is the former Chief Economic Advisor to the former President of Guinea Alpha Conde. Dr. Doumbouya was the Minister of Budget of Guinea from 2016 to 2018. He has led the CEoG book project, Financing African Economies from Within. He is an economist and expert in economic development, banking, and monetary policy. As the former Minister Counsellor to the former President of Guinea, Dr. Doumbouya oversaw the establishment of clear financial reform expectations in the area of public financial management and monitored progress in these areas. Prior to joining the Guinean administration, Dr. Doumbouya taught Economics at the University of Ottawa, Canada.

Trudi Makhaya

Ms. Trudi Makhaya served as the Economic Advisor to President Cyril Ramaphosa from 2018 to 2023. From 2003 to 2010, she worked at Deloitte, Genesis Analytics, and AngloGold Ashanti in South Africa. Between 2010 and 2014, Trudi was an Economist and a Member of the Executive Committee at the Competition Commission of South Africa. In 2015, she founded an advisory firm focused on competition policy and entrepreneurship. She holds an MBA and an MSc in Development Economics from Oxford University.

Abdallah Msa

Dr. Abdallah Msa has more than forty years of experience in the evaluation, analysis, development, implementation, and monitoring of sectoral and global development policies. His doctoral training in economic analysis, along with his experience in significant roles and missions both in his country and at the African Union Commission and the African Development Bank, have strengthened his expertise in the evaluation and monitoring of development policies and programs/projects, particularly in Africa. He served as a government consultant in economic and financial matters and as Chief Government Economist at the Presidency of the Union of the Comoros from February 2018 to February 2023. He also served as Executive Director/Board Member at the African Development Bank from 2013 to 2016.

Sen Narrainen

Dr. Streevarsen Narrainen has been a Senior Economic Advisor at the Ministry of Finance and Economic Development (MOFED) since 2003. He served as a Senior Economic Advisor to the Prime Minister of Mauritius between 1996 and 2000 and as an Economic Advisor at MOFED between 1989 and 1996. Prior to 1989, he was an Assistant Professor of Economics at the University of Winnipeg and the University of Manitoba in Canada. He holds a PhD in Economics from McGill University in Montreal, Canada, specializing in Monetary Theory and Policy. He has been a member of the Monetary Policy Committee of the Bank of Mauritius since March 2015.

Stephane Ouedraogo

Mr. Stephane Ouedraogo is the former Special Advisor to the President of Burkina Faso in charge of Finance, Economic, and Investment Matters, a role he held from 2016 to 2022. In his previous position, he provided strategic orientation on economic, development, and policy plans at the national and regional levels and participated in the conception and funding mobilization of the National Economic Development Plan. Prior to that position, he worked in management at Arysta Life Science for West and Central Africa. He holds an MBA in Finance and Information Systems from Pace University in New York.

Amina Rwakunda

Mrs. Amina Umulisa Rwakunda is the former Chief Economist at the Ministry of Finance and Economic Development of Rwanda. She is a Board Director of the Rwanda Stock Exchange (RSE) and a Board Director of the National Institute of Statistics Rwanda (NISR). Mrs. Rwakunda is an experienced economist and a seasoned negotiator on regional integration matters, having served as the Deputy Chief Negotiator for Rwanda's High-Level Task Force on the East African Community (EAC) Monetary Union. She is also involved in negotiations on fiscal-related policies. Mrs. Rwakunda holds a master's degree in development economics from the University of Antwerp, Belgium.

Acronyms and Abbreviations

AAAA: Addis Ababa Action Agenda
AfCFTA: African Continental Free Trade Area Agreement
AfDB: African Development Bank
AML: Anti-money laundering
AMTs: Alternative minimum taxes
ANSD: National Agency for Statistics and Demography
ASYCUDA: Automated System for Customs Data
ATAF: African Tax Administration Forum
AU: African Union
AUC: African Union Commission

BEPS: Base erosion and profit shifting
BO: Beneficial ownership
BOM: Bank of Mauritius

CbcR: Country-by-country reporting
CBT Technical Committee: Cross-Border Taxation Technical Committee
CEMAC: Economic and Monetary Community of Central Africa
CEPS: Customs, Excise and Preventive Service
CFT: Combating the Financing of Terrorism
CGP: Africa Co-Guarantee Platform
CIT: Corporate income tax
CRSE: Commission De Régulation Du Secteur De l'Énergie
CSR: Corporate social responsibility

DBM Development Bank of Mauritius
DEM: Development and Enterprise Market
DGI: Directorate-General of Taxes *(Direction Générale Des Impôts)*
DGID: Directorate General of Taxation and Domains

DRM Domestic resource mobilization
DVLA: Driver and Vehicle Licensing Authority

EBMs: Electronic billing machines
ECOWAS: Economic Community of West African States
ESG: Environmental, social, and governance
EU European Union

FDI: Foreign direct investment
fintech: financial technology
FSC: Financial Services Commission
FTA: Forum on Tax Administration

GDP: Gross Domestic Product
GDS: Gross Domestic Savings
GRA: Ghana Revenue Authority
GSMA: Global System for Mobile Communications Association

HNWIs: High-net-worth individuals

ICRTIC: Independent Commission for Reform of International Corporate Tax
ICT: Information and communication technologies
IF: G20/OECD Inclusive Framework for BEPS Implementation
IFFs: Illicit financial flows
IMF: International Monetary Fund
IPO: Initial public offerings
IRS: Internal Revenue Service
ITTI: Inventory of Tax Technology Initiatives

MHC: Mauritius Housing Company
MIC: Mauritius Investment Company
MNCs: multinational corporations
MNEs: multinational enterprises
MOBAA: Mauritius Offshore Business Activities Authority
MTRS: Medium-Term Revenue Strategy

NPF: National Pensions Fund

OECD: Organisation for Economic Co-operation and Development

PAPSS: Pan-African Payment and Settlement System
PCT: Platform for Collaboration on Tax
PPPs: Public-private partnerships
PSE: Plan Sénégal Émergent

RA-GAP: Revenue Administration Gap Analysis Program
RECs: Regional Economic Commissions
RRA: Rwanda Revenue Authority

SADC: Southern African Development Community
SBM: State Bank of Mauritius
SEM: Stock Exchange of Mauritius
SENELEC: National Electricity Company of Senegal
  (*Société Nationale d'Electricité du Sénégal*)
SICOM: State Insurance Company of Mauritius
SIGA: State Interest and Governance Authority
SMEs: Medium-Sized Enterprises
SOE: State-owned enterprise
SSA: Sub-Saharan African
SSNIT: Social Security and National Insurance Trust

TADAT: Tax Administration Diagnostic Assessment Tool
TCR: Regional Cooperation Tax
TIN: Taxpayer Identification Number
TIWB: Tax Inspectors Without Borders

UNCTAD: United Nations Conference on Trade and Development
URA: Uganda Revenue Authority

VAT: Value-added tax
VATS: VAT Service

Foreword

Africa stands at a critical moment in history: leaving behind the scars of recent shocks – financial crises, pandemics, and aid cuts – and improving macroeconomic management to build a prosperous future for its 1.5 billion people. To build prosperity, the continent needs to grow faster, sustain it for decades and ensure that no one is left behind. This will require massive investments – both public and private. With official development assistance declining, external debt levels remaining elevated, and access to international financial markets becoming increasingly difficult and costly, financing the necessary investments would have to be sourced from within.

This book, *Financing African Economies from Within*, provides a timely, insightful, and solutions-oriented analysis of how domestic resource mobilization can serve as the engine for sustainable development across Africa. It is premised on the recognition that for Africa to really develop, it must harness the power of its institutions, capital, and people. It offers a comprehensive roadmap for how African countries can build robust, self-financed economies. It examines the essential contributions of the private sector and identifies the structural and policy barriers that have stifled deeper financial development. From infrastructure gaps to limited access to finance, and from governance challenges to political uncertainty, the book candidly diagnoses the issues. But more importantly, it provides concrete, evidence-based strategies for overcoming them. Drawing on powerful case studies – such as Mauritius's phased path to financial self-sufficiency and Rwanda's successful digital tax reforms – the book illustrates how innovation, policy consistency, and institutional reform can generate lasting impact. It also delves into the growing potential of digitalization to enhance tax administration, broaden the revenue base, and improve accountability. Importantly, it does not shy away from complex regional and global challenges, such as unproductive tax incentives, profit shifting by multinationals, and the uneven power dynamics in international tax negotiations.

Africa needs bold, informed, and independent thought leadership to shape economic policies that serve its people. This book embodies that vision. It challenges outdated paradigms, repositions the domestic private sector as a primary engine of growth, and proposes actionable frameworks to catalyze infrastructure investment and capital formation. It emphasizes that sustainable progress lies not in circumventing governance challenges, but in confronting them through stronger institutions, better fiscal management, and innovative partnerships.

The book is particularly distinguished by its authorship. Written by Chief Economic Advisors to Heads of States across Africa, it reflects the collective wisdom, experience, and policy leadership of a network of professionals who have advised African governments at the highest level. The insights offered in this book are informed by years of direct involvement in macroeconomic planning, budget formulation, investment strategy, and structural reform implementation. They are shaped by the urgent questions faced in cabinet rooms, and the hard-earned lessons drawn from advising finance ministers, presidents, and prime ministers. This book – the first in the series – by the Chief Economist of Government (CEoG) is a testament to the critical role that a network of senior policy advisors can offer to shaping policymaking in the region. The network provides a platform for peer learning, thought leadership, and African voices on global, regional, and local issues relevant to African development. It is our hope that the network grows to become the premier platform where thought leadership meets policy experience, and beneficial to all, particularly, upcoming policy advisors in the region.

Finally, *Financing African Economies from Within* is more than a book; it is a call to action. It reminds us that with the right policies, institutions, and leadership, Africa can finance its own development, on its own terms. It is our hope that this work inspires policymakers, development partners, scholars, and citizens to commit to a new chapter in Africa's economic journey – one where domestic resource, not foreign aid, are the foundation of prosperity.

Andrew Dabalen
Chief Economist,
Africa Region
The World Bank

Albert Zeufack
Division Director,
Angola, Burundi, DRC and STP,
Former Africa Chief Economist
The World Bank

Preface

In the dynamic and ever-evolving landscape of global economics, the African continent stands at a pivotal juncture. The quest for sustainable development and economic self-reliance has never been more critical. This seminal book, *Financing African Economies from Within*, is a culmination of experiences, insights, and lessons learned from critical positions in government, particularly as advisors to heads of state. This book is the first of its kind, written by advisors to African heads of state or African governments and it is the first from the Chief Economists of Government (CEoG) initiative. It is also a reflection of the collective wisdom of the advisors to heads of state or government, garnered through peer learning and the shared experiences of African policymakers and development practitioners.

The motivation behind this book stems from a deep-seated belief in the potential of African economies to thrive through internally driven strategies and solutions. As advisors to heads of state, we have witnessed firsthand the challenges of implementing policies aimed at domestic resources to finance African economies. This book seeks to provide a comprehensive understanding of these experiences, offering valuable lessons and practical insights for current and future leaders.

The intended audience includes policymakers, development practitioners, academics, and anyone with a vested interest in the development and financing of African economies. From this book, readers can expect to gain a nuanced understanding of the intricacies involved in financing development from within, as well as the key lessons learned from various countries across the continent. The contributions from key actors in the development of their respective countries provide a rich tapestry of knowledge and experience that is both informative and inspiring.

We extend our heartfelt thanks to all the contributors who, despite their busy schedules, took the time to share their invaluable insights and experiences. Their dedication and commitment to the development of Africa are truly commendable. Special thanks are also due to the Think Africa Partnership and the CEoG

Secretariat for their unwavering support in bringing this book to fruition. Their contributions have been instrumental in making this project a reality.

It is our hope that this book will serve as a valuable resource and a source of inspiration for all those committed to the development financing of African economies.

Executive Summary

Leveraging the African private sector in financing development

The private sector in Africa accounts for 80 percent of total production, two-thirds of total investment, and 75 percent of lending, though it lags other regions in domestic resource mobilization.[1] Banking assets represent less than 60 percent of GDP, and financial market development is limited, with a dominance of retail banks and a lack of debt and equity instruments. Progress has been made, with the presence of stock exchanges in 29 African countries, increased private equity fundraising, and a growing African bond market. The sector is also constrained by several factors, including limited access to financing, inefficient transport networks, lack of access to electricity, governance-related limitations, corruption, and political instability.

Governments account for a significant portion of infrastructure investments in Africa, while private financing is relatively low. Insufficient infrastructure leads to a loss in GDP growth (around 2 percent in annual GDP growth) and hinders intraregional trade. Bridging the infrastructure gap requires an annual investment of US$93 billion and increased private sector involvement. To engage the private sector, enabling frameworks must be strengthened, innovative financing mechanisms should be explored, and digital banking and mining sectors can be leveraged. Addressing sector-specific challenges and promoting local content in infrastructure projects are also important considerations. These efforts can unlock Africa's economic potential and foster sustainable growth.

The case study of Mauritius showcases how the private sector can significantly contribute to a country's development agenda by overcoming constraints and leveraging public policy support to drive nation-building. Mauritius, which was dependent on sugar exports to finance its development, managed to achieve self-sufficiency in development finance through various strategies and phases. After gaining independence, building on the capital accumulated by sugar exporters, the country maintained high national savings for decades, providing a solid

---

1 Domestic resource mobilization includes the development of capital markets which can provide finance in local currency at lower rates, eliminating risks from currency fluctuations.

foundation for financing the diversification of the economy. Although there has been a decline in the savings-to-GDP ratio in recent years, the country's well-established banking sector and monetized economy at the time of independence have contributed to its ability to achieve self-sufficiency. This demonstrates the importance of expanding the financial system and having a strong foundation in place.

The establishment of self-sufficiency in development finance in Mauritius can be divided into three phases. The first phase, from 1965 to 1990, focused on state control and building institutional capacity. The government implemented direct control measures on bank lending to prioritize credit for key sectors, resulting in significant improvement in banking system monetization. The second phase, from 1991 to 2010, emphasized expanding the non-banking financial sector and capital markets, with a shift towards liberalization and reforms aimed at enhancing efficiency in resource allocation. The third phase, from 2011 to the present, has focused on inclusiveness, efficiency, and internalization, with an emphasis on providing finance access to diverse segments of the population and developing the equity financing sector.

While capital market development has improved in several African countries in recent years, its contribution to internal financing is not yet fulfilled. South Africa has a paradoxical situation where it has one of the most developed financial markets in the world but low rates of fixed capital formation, constraining its contribution to growth. The equity market, dominated by the Johannesburg Stock Exchange (JSE), is deep and liquid, with a market capitalization/GDP ratio exceeding that of other emerging markets, and even advanced economies like the United States and Republic of Korea.

To address this paradox, South Africa has introduced mechanisms like the Budget Facility for Infrastructure and the Infrastructure Fund. These initiatives aim to enhance project preparation, improve the project pipeline, and attract private investment. Regulatory changes, such as modifications to pension fund regulations, have been implemented to encourage infrastructure investment. Public-private partnerships (PPPs) have also been emphasized, with a need to simplify approval processes and reform the policy framework to encourage private sector financing solutions.

Leveraging digital technologies to improve domestic resource mobilization

In recent years, there has been a growing trend towards the modernization of customs and tax administration in Africa through the adoption of electronic filing and tax payment systems. Electronic filing was available for tax and/or customs declarations in 23 SSA countries out of 48 in 2022, with implementation in progress in 6 other countries. Additionally, electronic tax payment was available in 19 SSA countries. These digital services allow taxpayers to file their taxes electronically and make online payments, resulting in increased tax performance, reduced opportunities for corruption, and improved transparency. Adopting digital technologies in tax administration also improves the efficiency of tax collection, leading to cost and time savings. For example, in Guinea, tax revenues on international trade increased by 151.6 percent just 8 months after the adoption of this technology. Taxation of digital transactions offers a promising way to increase tax revenue and target tax avoidance. South Africa, for instance, has raised about US$929 million since implementing its cross-border VAT on electronic services in 2014.

Taxation of the digital economy is a promising avenue for increasing tax revenue. This can be achieved by broadening the base of value-added tax (VAT) or sales taxes, or by introducing new direct digital service taxes. The digital revolution offers significant revenue generation potential, particularly as e-commerce revenue is expected to grow substantially in African countries. The use of electronic billing machines can automate transaction capture and reduce the risk of fraud and tax disputes. Some African countries, such as Côte d'Ivoire, Ghana, The Republic of Congo, Uganda, and Zimbabwe, already tax digital financial services through excise taxes on money transfers. While imposing levies on mobile money may raise concerns about financial inclusion, it can generate short-term revenue. SSA leads in mobile money usage, with a significant share of transactions occurring through mobile money platforms.

However, digitalization also presents challenges for tax systems, especially tax challenges related to profit shifting, VAT collection on cross-border trade, and the taxation of digital financial assets. The growth of the digital economy raises questions about how to allocate taxing rights on income generated from cross-border activities among jurisdictions. The digital economy also eases profit shifting to low-tax jurisdictions, posing difficulties for countries to protect their tax bases. African tax systems were not designed for cryptocurrencies, and the lack of adequate legislation for taxing digital services limits countries' ability to leverage e-commerce opportunities. Inadequate infrastructure, connectivity, and low digital skills among users further hinder the potential gains from digital technology adoption in Africa. Efforts are needed to address these challenges and harness the full potential of digitalization in the region. International cooperation through tax negotiations and information sharing plays a crucial role in finding innovative solutions to these challenges.

Although digitalizing tax administrations offers several advantages, critical environmental barriers in Africa limit its vast potential. The success of the customs and tax administration's modernization heavily depends on the environment. The lack of appropriate infrastructure and internet connectivity, digital literacy and training, confidence in the government, adoption by tax officials and taxpayers, and adequate legislation and political leadership are major constraints to the effectiveness of technology reforms in African countries.

Improving electricity supply and internet connectivity is essential to facilitate the adoption of digital technologies. Information and communications technology (ICT) reforms must be supported by introducing new and appropriate legal and regulatory frameworks inspiring users' trust and confidence in the integrity and security of the systems, notably concerning the privacy and safety of data. The new regulation must also cover data sharing between revenue authorities. Investment in human resources is crucial to ensure tax officers' effective and proper use of digital tools. In addition, it is crucial that governments invest in education and training to ensure that citizens take up digital technology. Illustrative case studies focused on Rwanda, Guinea, and the Democratic Republic of Congo (DRC) present the experiences of these countries in modernizing customs and tax administrations.

Guinea embarked on a digitalization journey, starting with customs procedures to address underperformance in domestic revenue mobilization. The implementation of the Electronic Single Window system resulted in a significant increase in taxes on international trade. Eight months after adopting the technology, tax revenues from international trade had increased by 151.6 percent. Over the next eight months, trade tax revenues continued to rise at a rate of 31.5 percent. These positive results were achieved through improved customs administration performance, time and cost savings, reduced in-person interactions, and enhanced fraud detection enabled by digital tools. While the increase in revenue has been smaller in recent years, the activation of additional features of the digital platform, such as the ability to pay taxes through mobile money transactions, is expected to further boost government revenue. The digitalization of customs procedures in Guinea demonstrates the potential of digital tools to enhance revenue authorities' performance, improve public service delivery, increase transparency and accountability, and reduce corruption.

Rwanda has undergone a comprehensive digital transformation in its tax administration, aiming to modernize the Rwanda Revenue Authority (RRA) and make it customer-centric, data driven, and IT-powered. The digitalization of the tax system in Rwanda began in 2004 with the introduction of off-the-shelf software for taxpayer data management and has been followed by implementation of an Automated System for Customs Data (ASYCUDA) to streamline customs procedures. Improved access to internet with the fiber optic network rolled out in 2010 and measures aiming at improving digital literacy and the adaptation of technology were also determinant. The introduction of electronic billing machines (EBMs) reduced fraudulent VAT claims and improved the accuracy and transparency of transaction data. The RRA has also adopted a data-driven operating model, using analytics and automated audit case selection to enhance audit efficiency and risk-based interventions.

Rwanda's digitalization efforts yielded significant improvements in revenue collection, and efficiency, with a tax-to-GDP ratio increasing from 11.2 percent in 2009/10 to 16.0 percent in 2019/20. The number of registered taxpayers increased fivefold between 2011 and 2019, and e-filing and e-payment systems are widely used. The advanced digital infrastructure and systems enabled taxpayers to fulfil their obligations seamlessly during the Covid-19 pandemic. Beyond revenue collection, the use of technology in taxation has provided valuable data for decision-making and policy formulation. Insights from electronic billing machines have shaped trade and industrial policies, and the data have been used for economic analysis, and coordination of fiscal and monetary policies. The fusion of technology and governance has improved the business climate, fostered collaboration between the government and the private sector, and reduced opportunities for corruption and the cost of compliance.

Governance and the mobilization of internal resources

To reduce their reliance on aid, sub-Saharan African countries have been adopting reforms to strengthen tax and non-tax revenue mobilization. Although tax revenues are relatively low in comparison with Latin American countries and high-income countries, over the past decade, there has been a shift towards increasing the tax-to-GDP ratio. Several factors have contributed to recent progress in revenue mobilization, including economic growth, which expands the tax base and increases revenue generation. Simplification of tax codes, modernization of tax systems, and efforts to strengthen tax administrations and encourage tax compliance have also played a role in reducing tax evasion and avoidance. However, significant untapped revenue potential remains, as the IMF estimates that the median country in Africa could increase its tax-to-GDP ratio by 3 to 5 percent.

In Senegal, the reform program is integrated into a broader development agenda called *Plan Sénégal Émergent (PSE)*.[2] The government has prioritized domestic revenue mobilization as a central component of the PSE. Key object-

---

2 The PSE aims to achieve the country's development aspirations by 2035 and emphasizes structural reforms, infrastructure development, and private sector growth.

ives include increasing tax performance and broadening the tax base to reach a tax-to-GDP ratio of 20 percent by 2023. The government also implemented transparency measures, such as the adoption of the Code of Transparency in Public Finance Management and securing membership in the Global Forum on Transparency and Exchange of Information for Tax Purposes. One specific area of focus in Senegal is property taxation. Despite its revenue potential, property taxes in Senegal perform poorly. The government implemented reforms to improve the collection of property taxes, including a census program of properties throughout the country.

Ghana implemented key measures to improve tax and non-tax revenue mobilization, starting with the establishment of the Ghana Revenue Authority (GRA) in 2009. The GRA allowed for the harmonization of the activities of three independent, semi-autonomous revenue agencies, aligning revenue mobilization strategies and modernizing revenue administration. The launch of the Ghana Beyond Aid program in 2019 further emphasizes self-sufficiency, economic transformation, and sustainable development. Revenue measures include enhancing the efficiency of revenue collection agencies, identifying potential taxpayers, enforcing tax payments (especially in the mining sector), curbing corruption, improving efficiency in state-owned enterprises, and optimizing expenditure and public investments. To increase the tax-to-GDP ratio to 23 percent by 2028, Ghana also implemented initiatives such as the national digital address system and the national identification system to incorporate more individuals and businesses into the tax net.

Cameroon has implemented multiple initiatives to mobilize domestic revenues, although its strategies are more fragmented compared to Senegal and Ghana. The key challenges in Cameroon's revenue mobilization efforts include addressing the high burden of tax expenditure, harnessing the revenue potential of the informal sector, and boosting individual contributions to revenue mobilization. The Tax Code has been amended to address these challenges. In tackling the informal sector, the government has strengthened the withholding tax mechanism, allowing tax deductions to be made on transactions conducted by informal sector enterprises with large enterprises. The traceability of cash transactions has also been improved, with restrictions on corporate tax deductions and VAT deductions for cash payments exceeding certain thresholds. These measures have increased the taxable population by 58 percent. As for Senegal, efforts are being made to register more taxpayers, particularly targeting those with potential contributions through property taxes. The Directorate General of Taxes has developed a three-year plan for 2023 to 2025 to modernize the tax system in response to findings from the Tax Administration Diagnostic Assessment Tool and IMF recommendations.

State-owned enterprises (SOEs) in Africa, particularly in Senegal, Cameroon, and Ghana, face challenges in contributing to domestic revenue mobilization. While SOEs are expected to generate revenues by providing essential goods and services, they often struggle with inefficiency, corruption, and mismanagement. Reforms have been implemented to address these challenges, including privatization, restructuring, and downsizing of SOEs. In Senegal, SOEs such as Air Senegal and Senelec have faced financial difficulties. Air Senegal has struggled to make investments profitable, but reforms and a change in leadership have led to a reduction in revenue losses. Senelec, on the other hand, has undergone comprehensive restructuring and now generates revenues that contribute to government income. To reduce losses, performance contracts have been introduced in Cameroon, while in Ghana, the government established the State Interest and Governance Authority (SIGA) to monitor SOEs' performance and provide guidance and support. SIGA's efforts have helped reduce SOEs' losses, and some companies have paid dividends to the state.

From tax competition to cooperation?

African countries face obstacles in preserving their tax bases, including unproductive tax incentives, inadequate taxation of natural resources, and profit shifting through controlled transactions. To address these challenges and reduce tax competition, better cooperation and coordination are necessary. Steps such as harmonizing tax policies, establishing regional tax authorities, and improving information sharing can create a more level playing field for investment and generate more revenue for governments.

The current international tax regime, primarily led by the Organisation for Economic Co-operation and Development (OECD) and the G20, has inadequacies that need to be addressed. The Two-Pillar Solution proposed by the OECD includes measures to ensure multinational corporations pay their fair share of taxes and prevent profit shifting. However, concerns have been raised by the African Tax Administration Forum (ATAF) regarding the reallocation of profits to market jurisdictions and the minimum global tax rate, which they argue should be higher to reduce profit shifting out of Africa. In addition, there are challenges for Africa in implementing the proposed measures. These include implementation challenges due to complex tax systems and limited administrative capacity, political resistance from countries reliant on low tax rates, limited scope in addressing domestic tax evasion and corruption, limited benefits for countries with few multinational corporations, and the rapid pace of change in international tax standards. The existing global tax framework, particularly the proposed Pillar I and Pillar II measures, may also not fully address broader issues such as corruption and weak enforcement of regulations in Africa's extractive industries.

The adoption of the UN resolution on tax cooperation signifies a shift towards more inclusive tax governance, with the aim of creating a framework convention on tax. This move proposes transferring global tax rule decision-making from the OECD to the UN, indicating a global consensus for more equitable tax governance. However, there are risks associated with the potential loss of sovereignty and the dominance of developed nations' interests in the global tax agenda. To ensure the implementation of the UN resolution benefits Africa, it is crucial to address power imbalances, improve information exchange, and support African countries in developing the necessary capacity to participate effectively in international tax cooperation. Efforts must be made to give African countries an equal voice in the development of international tax rules and to address the root causes of illicit financial flows, such as corruption and weak governance.

Regional tax coordination can complement global tax reform by addressing regional profit shifting and tax competition pressures. Regional initiatives can leverage similarities in economic structures, administrative capacity, and culture to facilitate agreement on issues such as a regional minimum tax rate. This can lead to greater cooperation and coordination among African nations on tax matters, promoting inclusive and effective tax governance. The African Union Commission's (AUC) Tax Strategy for Africa can provide a framework for African countries to develop tax standards aligned with the principles outlined in the UN resolution and ensure African perspectives are considered in international tax discussions. Additionally, the African Continental Free Trade Area (AfCFTA) and regional initiatives like the ECOWAS Common External Tariff (CET) Regime and the Africa Co-Guarantee Platform (CGP) also contribute to reducing tax competition and promoting cooperation. The AfCFTA's deeper regional integration can stimulate local production, expand the taxable base, and enhance domestic resource mobilization in Africa.

CHAPTER 1

Role of the African Private Sector in Financing Development

1.1. Introduction

The private sector contributes 80 percent of total production, two thirds of total investment, and 75 percent of lending within the continent's economy. It thus plays an important role as a source of funding for public goods and productive capacity within the economy, alongside the role played by external funders, including development partners and foreign investors. It is important to note that domestic resource mobilization (DRM) goes beyond the optimization of taxation and other government levies, foundational as these are to development. In fact, DRM is defined as the "generation of savings domestically, as opposed to investment, loans, grants or remittances received from external sources, and their allocation to socially productive investments within the country" (AfDB and Development Centre of the OECD, 2010, p.79). Private domestic savings are channeled by the financial sector (e.g., private banks) towards investment, whereas public resource mobilization or public savings emanate from the excess of public revenues over current government expenditure (AfDB and Development Centre of the OECD, 2010).

Sub-Saharan Africa (SSA) has one of the lowest savings rates among developing regions, averaging 19 percent between 2010 and 2021. In contrast, East Asia's savings rate during the same period was 37 percent, contributing to its leading investment rates among developing regions. From 2000 to 2017, SSA's average savings rate was 22 percent, compared to 34 percent in East Asia and 27 percent in South Asia. Alarmingly, SSA's savings rate dropped from 27 percent in 2006 to 19 percent in 2017. To foster economic growth in the region, it is crucial to implement policies that significantly boost domestic savings rates (Sena, 2023).

The Addis Ababa Action Agenda recognizes the role of the private sector in financing development. It commits to enabling private sector action:

> We will develop policies and, where appropriate, strengthen regulatory frameworks to better align private sector incentives with public goals, including incentivizing the private sector to adopt sustainable practices, and foster long term quality investment. Public policy is needed to create the enabling environment at all levels and a regulatory framework necessary to encourage entrepreneurship and a vibrant domestic sector.[3]

Domestic resource mobilization also encompasses the development and deepening of capital markets that can advance finance in local currency at lower rates. The mobilization of resources within the domestic economy has distinct advantages over foreign flows. Because the funds are largely denominated in local currency, this eliminates the risks and distortions that arise from currency fluctuations. The ability to raise funds from the local private sector also serves as a signal for other resource flows, ultimately helping the country to optimize its sources of finance.

Nevertheless, the role of the private sector in resource mobilization in Africa lags behind other regions. Banking assets represent less than 60 percent of GDP on the continent, compared with more than 100 percent in other emerging and advanced economies. In addition, domestic resource mobilization is limited by constraints to financial market development. The financial services sector is dominated by retail banks that do not offer the full range of services. Furthermore, capital markets do not offer the full range of debt and equity instruments required by the business sector. [4]

There has been some progress, however, as 29 African countries have stock exchanges, compared to 5 in 1989. Proceeds from initial public offerings (IPO) in Africa between 2014 and 2019 were US$27.1 billion, less than 1.4 percent of global IPO flows in that period. Private equity fundraising in Africa increased to US$2.7 billion in 2018. The African bond market was valued at US$500

3 A/RES/69/313- Addis Ababa Action Agenda of the Third International Conference on Financing for Development (Addis Ababa Action Agenda) 36: https://sustainabledevelopment.un.org/topics/finance/decisions.
4 AU (2021): https://au.int/en/pressreleases/20211108/leveraging-private-sector-engagement-africa-we-want; UNECA (2020): https://www.uneca.org/sites/default/files/fullpublicationfiles/ERA_2020_mobile_20201213.pdf

billion in 2019 with local currency bonds making up 78 percent of outstanding debt in Africa.[5]

Recognizing the foundational importance of policies that support both private and public savings, this chapter examines the private sector in Africa and proposes strategies that could be put in place not only to improve the contribution of African banks, institutional investors, and other private sector actors to development financing but also and above all to involve the domestic private sector in infrastructure financing.

1.2. Mapping of the African private sector landscape

1.2.1. Characteristics of the private sector in Africa

The private sector in Africa is a significant driver of economic growth and has the potential to elevate economies from low-income to middle-income status. Globally, the private sector generates over 70 percent of jobs, produces goods and services, and contributes more than 80 percent of government revenue in low-income and middle-income countries through taxes. However, in Africa, limited access to financing is identified as the most critical challenge for businesses. Approximately 19 percent of small firms and 14 percent of medium-sized firms consider it the main obstacle to conducting business (UNECA, 2020).

1.2.1.1. Informality

The private sector in Africa has unique characteristics. One is the informality of companies, which is becoming increasingly important. Informal employment is the primary source of employment in Africa, constituting 85.8 percent of total employment and providing opportunities for numerous young job seekers on the continent (ILO, 2018). However, there are significant variations within the region, influenced by socio-economic development and the varying levels of informal employment. The informal economy accounts for 67.3 percent in Northern Africa and 89.2 percent in SSA (ILO, 2020).

The main reasons why companies in Africa choose not to formalize their existence include the fear of having to pay taxes, the lack of information about registration procedures, the cost of such procedures, and the feeling that they have nothing to gain by entering the formal sector. A survey conducted by Afrobarometer in 18 African countries in 2019–2020, suggests that most Africans believe their governments have the right to collect taxes. However,

---

5 With most of local currency bonds held by domestic investors. For example, in South Africa, 62 percent of local currency bonds are held by domestic investors.

support for taxation has weakened over the past decade, accompanied by a perception that people often evade paying taxes. Many Africans also question the fairness of the tax burden and express skepticism about their governments' use of tax revenues for the wellbeing of citizens. While most Africans are willing to pay higher taxes for youth support and national development, they face difficulties in accessing tax information and view tax officials as corrupt and untrustworthy. These perceptions potentially impact citizens' support for and compliance with tax administration.[6]

The formal sector in Africa is dominated by small businesses, especially in low-income countries. Although more prevalent in middle-income countries, medium and large enterprises, which account for only a third of business, are much less numerous in Africa than in other regions of the world. Although their contribution to total output is marginal, micro and small enterprises account for the largest number of enterprises on the continent and are also the main source of employment and income for the poor.

1.2.1.2. Other characteristics

The private sector in Africa exhibits several other key characteristics that shape its overall landscape, including:

- *Growing entrepreneurship*: Africa is experiencing a surge in entrepreneurship, with a vibrant ecosystem of startups and small and medium-sized enterprises (SMEs). These enterprises play a vital role in driving innovation, job creation, and economic growth across various sectors.
- *Diverse industries*: The private sector in Africa spans a wide range of industries, including agriculture, manufacturing, telecommunications, financial services, technology, and renewable energy. There is a growing emphasis on sectors such as digital technology, e-commerce, and renewable energy, driven by the continent's young and tech-savvy population.
- *Foreign direct investment (FDI)*: Africa continues to attract foreign direct investment from both traditional and emerging markets. FDI flows into sectors like infrastructure development, natural resources, and manufacturing. These investments contribute to job creation, technology transfer, and improved infrastructure.
- *Access to finance*: Access to finance remains a significant challenge for businesses in Africa. However, innovative financial technologies, mobile banking, and microfinance initiatives are expanding financial inclusion and improving

---

6 See Afrobarometer: https://www.afrobarometer.org/publication/ad428-troubling-tax-trends-fewer-africans -support-taxation-more-say-people-avoid-paying/.

access to capital for entrepreneurs and SMEs. For example, in the digital age, Ghana, Kenya, Rwanda, and Uganda are spearheading the fintech revolution to empower the unbanked population, including women entrepreneurs and youth-led small businesses (UNECA, 2020).

- *Public-private partnerships (PPPs)*: Collaboration between the private sector and governments through public-private partnerships is gaining momentum. These partnerships aim to address infrastructure gaps, improve service delivery, and promote sustainable development.

Of course, Africa is a diverse continent, and as such, the mentioned characteristics only provide a broad overview and vary across countries and regions.

1.2.2. Key challenges faced by the private sector in Africa

The private sector faces a similar set of barriers in all African countries, although the impact of these barriers varies according to the stage of national economic development. While the two main obstacles in low-income countries are electricity and access to finance, these factors are much less problematic in middle-income countries where skills gaps and labor regulations are the biggest challenges. Specifically, fundamental limitations, such as inefficient transport networks and lack of access to electricity and finance, are most critical in the poorest countries, while governance-related limitations, such as high levels of taxation and quality of tax administration, are relatively more detrimental to the least poor low-income countries. In middle-income countries, policy-induced limitations, such as skills shortages and labor regulations, weigh the most. Therefore, as countries develop, they begin to overcome basic barriers, but tend to be subsequently hampered by governance and public policy issues.

Barriers to private sector development also differ by type of business. Large companies are more concerned about corruption, lack of skills and labor regulations, while exporting companies place tax administration at the top of their list of concerns. These systemic factors are less troublesome for small businesses, which tend to be more aggrieved by the lack of access to finance (and its excessive cost), by the lack of collateral and by the lack of technical, accounting, and managerial skills of entrepreneurs, judging the lack of skills as less penalizing. For micro-enterprises in both middle- and low-income countries, the most significant barrier is the lack of access to finance, although micro-enterprises operating in middle-income countries also often complain about the cumbersome permitting and authorization procedures, which can be a determining factor in their decision to remain in the informal sector.

Some barriers become more significant as economies become more competitive. These include access to transport, access to finance, public order, tax administration, business permits, corruption, customs and trade regulations, and the judiciary. Furthermore, tax rates and access to electricity also become more inconvenient for businesses as a country's competitiveness improves. As a country moves from low to intermediate competitiveness, more companies register, making tax rates more problematic. Similarly, firms may face challenges in maintaining investment levels and improving capital intensity due to competitive pressures. This underscores the need for strategic investments in infrastructure, financial systems, and supportive policies to sustain growth and ensure that businesses can thrive in a more competitive environment.

Regarding corruption, approximately 6.3 percent of businesses in Africa face significant obstacles as a result. This hampers private sector growth and, consequently, economic development by deterring foreign investment, increasing business costs, compromising service quality, distorting competition, and promoting the improper allocation of limited resources. Larger firms face greater concerns with political instability and insecurity compared to smaller ones. Insecurity manifests in different ways, including civil wars, criminal violence, political unrest, and terrorism (UNECA, 2020). Africa is home to 20 out of the 37 most fragile states globally, as per the World Bank.[7] When a country is deemed risky, this discourages investors, leading to higher lending rates and difficulties in obtaining financing. This situation persists even when peace is restored, making it challenging to secure funding, especially for infrastructure reconstruction (Africa CEO Forum, 2014; UNCTAD, 2015).

The table below on gross domestic savings as a percentage of GDP from 2014 to 2023 reveals significant regional disparities in savings rates across Africa and other parts of the world. In Eastern and Southern Africa, savings rates have been relatively stable but moderate, fluctuating between 17.4 percent and 20.6 percent over the period, highlighting some resilience but also indicating a limited propensity to save compared to other regions. SSA, on the other hand, shows a concerning downward trend, with savings rates dropping from 21.3 percent in 2014 to a mere 4.7 percent in 2023, underscoring severe economic challenges and a critical need for policy interventions to boost savings and investment.

In contrast, East Asia and the Pacific consistently exhibits the highest savings rates, averaging around 37–39 percent, which helps to explain the region's robust investment rates and economic growth. Similarly, the Middle East and North

---

7 The FY23 list of fragile and conflict-affected countries is available here https://www.worldbank.org/en/topic/fragilityconflictviolence/brief/classification-of-fragile-and-conflict-affected-situations.

Africa, despite some volatility, maintains relatively high savings rates, ranging from 26.9 percent to 38.8 percent, indicating stronger financial systems and savings culture. South Asia, while experiencing a gradual decline, maintains moderate savings rates between 25.1 percent and 28.1 percent, still higher than those in SSA.

The limited savings base in regions like SSA can lead to a crowding-out effect, where government borrowing to finance fiscal deficits absorbs a significant portion of available savings, leaving less for private sector investment. This is particularly problematic when public deficits are driven by consumption rather than investment, as public consumption does not generate future income, unlike investment, which can enhance productivity and economic capacity. Therefore, high public consumption at the expense of private investment can constrain overall economic growth. This analysis highlights the need for African policymakers to implement strategies that enhance financial systems, promote savings, and balance public consumption with investment. Addressing these issues is crucial for sustainable economic development and improved financial resilience across the continent.

Table 1. Gross domestic savings (percent of GDP)

Region	2014	2015	2016	2017	2018	2019	2020	2021	2022	2023
Eastern & Southern Africa	19.3	17.4	17.5	18.6	18.4	18.9	18.9	20.6	20.2	17.6
East Asia & Pacific	37.2	37.4	36.9	37.5	37.6	36.9	37.3	39.1	39.5	38.1
Middle East & North Africa	36.9	29.4	29.2	31.5	34.5	32.4	26.9	32.5	38.8	36.3
Sub-Saharan Africa	21.3	17.6	14.2	11.1	12	14.6	13.1	12.2	12.6	4.7
South Asia	28.1	27.2	27.5	27.7	26.9	25.7	25.1	26	25.5	26.7

Source: World Development Indicators

Furthermore, the data on private capital investment, exits, and fundraising across different regions highlight several key challenges faced by the private sector in Africa (Table 2). While Africa has shown a substantial year-on-year increase in private capital investment (47 percent in 2021), it remains significantly lower in absolute terms compared to other regions like China and Southeast Asia. This disparity underscores the ongoing struggle of African markets to attract substantial private capital due to perceived higher risks and lower returns on investment. Moreover, the high variability and lower volumes of private capital exits (44 percent year-on-year change) indicate instability and potential issues in the liquidity and profitability of investments within the region. Additionally, the data on private capital fundraising reveal that Africa lags behind most regions, with a modest 29 percent increase in 2021. This relatively slow growth rate suggests difficulties in accessing and mobilizing financial resources for business expansion and innovation. In comparison, regions like Southeast Asia and the Asia-Pacific show more robust growth in fundraising, reflecting better-developed financial markets and stronger investor confidence.

As mentioned above, finance is crucial for the survival of the private sector, therefore, its limited availability hinders the growth of businesses in Africa. Small firms heavily rely on retained earnings or internal funds, which account for approximately 78 percent of their working capital. Medium-sized firms depend on internal funds for 73 percent of their working capital, while large firms rely on internal funds for 70 percent. In contrast, only 5 percent of small firms' working capital is financed by banks, whereas large firms receive approximately 13.7 percent of their working capital from banks, nearly three times the proportion of small firms (UNCTAD, 2015; UNECA, 2020).

Table 2. Private capital dynamics in Africa, 2017–2021 (US$ billion)

	2017	2018	2019	2020	2021	YoY change (%)
Private capital investment						
China	69.9	83.7	47.2	75.5	96.0	27
India	17.6	17.6	24.2	31.0	52.9	71
Southeast Asia	8.7	21.0	9.5	10.6	21.5	103
Latin America	10.1	12.6	15.6	16.8	29.4	75
Africa	3.4	4.2	3.9	4.3	6.3	47
CEE	7.1	3.9	3.3	2.4	11.5	379
Middle East	0.4	0.6	4.7	10.5	15.1	44
Private capital exits (outflows)						
China	17.8	40.8	18.4	55.9	51.4	-8
India	15.2	31.4	9.1	6.0	33.9	465
Southeast Asia	4.5	3.7	4.3	5.4	11.1	106
Latin America	7.5	7.3	10.7	15.4	17.6	14
Africa	1.1	3.8	11.6	1.8	2.6	44
CEE	3.8	4.4	1.2	7.8	8.2	5
Middle East	1.1	0.6	3.5	3.5	1.9	-46
Private capital fundraising						
Asia-Pacific*	58	84.2	70.0	69.0	88.3	28
China	16.4	37.3	29.8	27.4	36.4	33
India	5.4	8.1	6.7	4.9	5.7	16
Southeast Asia	1.9	1.3	2.9	2.1	2.9	38
Latin America	4.9	9.8	4.8	7.7	5.8	-25
Africa	2.7	3.2	3.4	2.4	3.1	29
CEE	1.3	1.8	1.8	1.8	1.7	-6

Middle East	0.2	0.1	0.4	0.4	0.4	0
Multi-Region	4.4	2.4	5.3	5.5	7.5	36

Source: GPCA. Data as of December 31, 2021 (https://www.globalprivatecapital.org/research/2022-global-private-capital -industry-data-analysis/)
Notes: (1) Exit totals include aggregate deal value and are not limited to disclosed distributions to private capital investors. (2) *Excludes funds dedicated to or predominantly investing in Japan, Australia and New Zealand. (3) Year-on-year (YoY) changes have been recalculated to correct for marginal differences between the figures as presented here and the original GPCA published data.

1.2.3. *Africa's private sector: Engine of growth and sustainability*

Despite facing challenges such as complex regulatory barriers, inequality, tax evasion,[8] intricate customs procedures, constraints on financial access, high transportation and logistics costs, and limited information access, the private sector in Africa continues to wield significant influence. Its development not only fuels economic growth but also drives infrastructure development, enhances tax revenue, and promotes financial inclusion. These positive impacts, however, necessitate a concerted effort to overcome the challenges (UNECA, 2023). Policymakers must strive for a balanced approach that encourages private sector growth while ensuring social responsibility, fairness, and compliance. Only then can the private sector's full potential as a contributor to sustainable development in Africa be realized.

1.2.3.1. *Economic growth*

Economic growth can reshape communities, enhance wellbeing, and empower individuals to flourish. However, to ensure that the most impoverished members of society reap the benefits of this growth, it must be paired with the creation of more quality jobs, which serve as one of the primary pathways out of poverty (Nishio, 2019). The private sector has been a vital engine for economic growth in Africa, contributing to increased GDP and job creation (AfDB, 2011). It also has the potential to directly contribute to achieving the SDGs and the African Union's Agenda 2063, through increasing productivity, creating jobs, and improving service delivery. In developing economies, over 90 percent of employment is generated by the private sector, encompassing both formal and informal roles. Even though most private businesses are small and face significant financial constraints that hinder their growth into large firms, SMEs are nonetheless vital

---

8 Tax evasion, in particular, poses a significant challenge as it undermines fair competition, reduces government revenue, and hampers economic development. Companies that evade taxes gain an unfair advantage over those that comply, distorting market dynamics and discouraging honest businesses. Furthermore, tax evasion leads to a shortfall in public funds, which are crucial for infrastructure development, public services, and social programs.

to African economies. They constitute around 90 percent of all private businesses and provide employment for more than 60 percent of the workforce in most African nations (UNECA, 2020). The growth of industries such as telecommunications, banking, and manufacturing has led to increased productivity and innovation.

1.2.3.2. *The private sector's key role in the AfCFTA*

The role of the private sector in regional trade, facilitated by the African Continental Free Trade Area (AfCFTA), can enhance competitiveness and foster development. Africa's vulnerability is in part due to its limited productive capacity, leading to a heavy dependence on imports for crucial goods. This dependence became evident during the Covid-19 pandemic when the continent faced difficulties in obtaining medical supplies, as over 90 percent are imported. Similarly, the suspension of wheat and corn exports from Russia and Ukraine during their conflict has led to food security issues in various African countries. Nonetheless, the AfCFTA is set to transform this scenario by unifying Africa into a single market worth US$2.7 trillion. By doing away with numerous trade barriers, the AfCFTA aims to diversify Africa's economy, thereby increasing its resilience against both natural and man-made shocks, including the effects of climate change. By utilizing financial technology (fintech) and engaging in regional value chains, the private sector enhances access to finance and increases the competitiveness of African businesses and interconnection in the African economy (UNECA, 2023; UNECA, 2020).

1.2.3.3. *Infrastructure development*

Infrastructure stands as Africa's most pressing developmental need, offering promising investment prospects for those willing to take a long-term position. Specifically, investments in power and energy infrastructure yield predictable and reliable returns, even in uncertain times, due to clear revenue streams backed by contractual agreements. These ensure a solid source of foreseeable cash flow. With the ongoing improvements in policy frameworks, procurement procedures, and a growing track record for private infrastructure projects, barriers to investment are diminishing, thus attracting more investors (AIIM, 2017).

Recent research by the IMF indicates that, by the end of the decade, the private sector has the potential to contribute additional yearly funding for both physical (roads, electricity) and social (health, education) infrastructure in SSA, amounting to 3 percent of the region's GDP. This equates to approximately US$50 billion annually (based on 2020 GDP figures) and nearly one-fourth of the prevailing average private investment ratio in the area, which stands at 13 percent of GDP (IMF, 2021).

Infrastructure development through public-private partnerships (PPPs) has been a significant trend in Africa. Projects like the Mombasa-Nairobi Standard Gauge Railway have not only improved transportation but also contributed to economic activity. In Kenya and the broader East Africa Region, this initiative is being championed as a tool to foster growth in sectors such as mining, oil, gas, energy, and commercial agriculture and connect countries like Uganda, Rwanda, Burundi, and South Sudan to the Indian Ocean's eastern trade routes. These development corridors hold the promise of significant socio-economic benefits including increased job opportunities, market accessibility, more efficient transportation, reduced food costs, and the integration of previously isolated regions (Patel, 2022; Gorecki, 2020). PPPs have enabled governments to leverage private capital and expertise to develop critical infrastructure.

1.2.3.4. Expansion of the tax base

In low- and middle-income countries, the private sector typically accounts for over 80 percent of government revenues. In Africa, there are more than 700 private businesses substantial enough to produce over US$500 million in annual revenue. Large corporations, defined as those with 100 or more employees, create yearly profits ranging from US$1 billion to US$1.4 trillion (UNECA, 2020).

Additionally, the private sector's support for entrepreneurship, particularly SMEs, is instrumental in fostering innovation and business growth. This, in turn, contributes to a wider tax base, enhancing the overall tax revenue essential for funding public services and infrastructure. In South Africa, for example, SMEs contribute around 34 percent of GDP and provide employment to about 60 percent of the labor force (IFC, 2018). This expansion has enhanced the country's tax revenue and fiscal sustainability.

1.2.3.5. Access to finance and innovation

Private sector development continues to improve access to finance. The rise of mobile banking and microfinance institutions has enabled financial inclusion for millions of Africans who previously lacked access to traditional banking services (World Bank, 2021). Serving as conduits for innovation and technology, private entities also foster skills development and capacity building. These contributions are essential in guaranteeing that Africa's emerging infrastructure not only functions at peak efficiency but also aligns with international standards (UNECA, 2019; AIIM, 2017).

1.3. How could the private sector play a role in financing Africa's development?

Amidst economic challenges that have emerged in the aftermath of the Covid-19 pandemic, Africa is confronting a significant test of the economic progress achieved over the past decade. Innovative financial instruments, practices, and policies are essential to facilitate substantial advancements across various business sectors. This includes start-ups, micro and small enterprises, social enterprises, professional businesses (such as lawyers and doctors), listed corporations, and public-private ventures. These businesses are vital for fostering inclusive economic growth, job creation, and improving livelihoods. (UNECA, 2020).

1.3.1 How can the contributions of African banks and institutional investors to financing development be improved?

Africa's sustainable development requires substantial financing, and to achieve this, it is crucial to harness the potential of banks and institutional investors (UNCTAD, 2021). These national financial entities play a pivotal role in channeling funds towards critical sectors and projects that drive economic growth and social development. To accelerate the contribution of banks and institutional investors to development financing in Africa, several key strategies can be implemented.

- Strengthening financial systems: This includes improving banking regulations, enhancing supervisory frameworks, and promoting financial sector stability. Robust financial systems attract investment, mitigate risks, and foster an enabling environment for banks and institutional investors to engage in development financing.
- Promoting financial inclusion: By expanding access to financial services, such as banking and insurance, to small and medium enterprises and underserved populations, the region can stimulate entrepreneurship, job creation, and economic empowerment. This can be achieved through innovative financial technology (fintech) solutions, mobile banking, and tailored financial products for marginalized segments of society.[9]
- Developing sustainable financial instruments: To attract banks and institutional investors, it is essential to develop sustainable financial instruments tailored to Africa's unique needs. Green bonds, social impact bonds, and infrastructure investment funds are examples of instruments that align financial returns with environmental and social objectives. These

---

9 World Economic Forum (2015) 'How the finance sector can drive Africa's economic growth', https://www.weforum.org/agenda/2015/06/how-the-finance-sector-can-drive-africas-economic-growth/

instruments attract socially responsible investors and enable financing for sustainable development projects, such as renewable energy, healthcare, and education (UNCTAD, 2021).

- Facilitating public-private partnerships (PPPs): PPPs provide a framework for collaboration between governments, banks, and institutional investors. By promoting PPPs, governments can leverage private sector expertise and resources to fund infrastructure and development projects. Clear legal and regulatory frameworks, risk-sharing mechanisms, and transparent procurement processes are essential for attracting banks and institutional investors to participate in PPPs.

- Strengthening governance and risk management: Banks and institutional investors prioritize well-governed environments with robust risk management frameworks. Enhancing governance structures, transparency, and accountability in African countries will instill confidence in financial institutions and promote financial stability. This can be achieved through effective regulatory oversight, anti-corruption measures, and strong legal frameworks that protect investors' rights. A significant area for attention is the governance of national social security institutions, which remains problematic in many African countries. These issues impact the financial stability and effectiveness of social security entities. Improving transparency, accountability, and efficiency within these institutions can ensure better management of social security funds, thereby contributing to sustainable development financing (International Social Security Association, 2021).

- Enhancing capacity building and knowledge sharing: To accelerate the contribution of banks and institutional investors, it is crucial to invest in capacity-building initiatives and knowledge-sharing platforms. This includes providing training and technical assistance to financial institutions, fostering partnerships with international organizations, and promoting research and data collection on development financing trends. Building local expertise and sharing best practices will strengthen the financial ecosystem and attract more banks and institutional investors.

- Driving innovation and technology transfer: The private sector can contribute to development by driving innovation and facilitating technology transfer. By investing in research and development, adopting new technologies, and collaborating with international partners, businesses can enhance productivity, create employment opportunities, and foster economic diversification. This, in turn, contributes to sustainable development and reduces dependence on traditional sectors.

- Real interest rates: Addressing the issue of real interest rates is crucial for development financing. High real interest rates can dissuade investment, reducing the ability of banks and institutional investors to channel savings into development projects. Lowering real interest rates to a level that encourages savings while remaining attractive to investors can help mobilize domestic resources more effectively. This approach not only stimulates economic activity but also provides a stable source of funds for long-term development initiatives (Yieke, 2023).

- Unfairness of credit rating agencies: African countries often face unfair treatment from credit rating agencies, resulting in higher borrowing costs and limited access to international capital markets. Addressing this unfair treatment by credit rating agencies is essential for improving Africa's access to international capital markets. This requires advocating for more equitable rating practices, ensuring accurate representation of economic realities by providing comprehensive and reliable data to counteract biases, and improving economic and financial governance to enhance creditworthiness. Furthermore, diversifying funding sources through the development of local capital markets and seeking alternative funding avenues can reduce dependency on external credit ratings, ultimately lowering borrowing costs and improving access to capital (APRM and UNECA, 2023).

In addition, the presence of well-functioning stock exchanges is another key element in accelerating development financing. Stock exchanges provide a platform for companies to raise capital and enable institutional investors to invest in viable projects. By promoting transparency, investor protection, and market efficiency, stock exchanges attract both domestic and international investors, facilitating the flow of funds into development initiatives. By implementing these measures, Africa can unlock the potential of its financial sector to drive sustainable and inclusive development across the continent.

1.3.2. How to attract the national private sector in infrastructure financing

Governments accounted for 37 percent of Africa's infrastructure investments in 2018, while private financing comprised only 11 percent. Insufficient infrastructure in Africa leads to an annual GDP growth loss of 2 percent. With adequate infrastructure, businesses could experience a 40 percent increase in productivity. Only 10 percent of trade in Africa occurs within the continent, compared to 70 percent in Europe and 50 percent in Asia. To bridge this gap, an annual investment of US$93 billion is required, equivalent to China's yearly investment in the past decade. Additionally, an annual investment of US$38 billion is necessary for electricity production for Africa to catch up (Africa CEO Forum, 2014; UNCTAD, 2015).

Limited government revenues have hindered infrastructure development, resulting in a substantial financing gap. Africa's infrastructure needs amounted to US\$130-170 billion annually up until 2025. Non-traditional donors, notably China, have played a significant role in bridging the gap, contributing over 25 percent of infrastructure funding on the continent. The energy and ICT sectors in Africa have attracted most of the private sector investment, representing over 90 percent of the total. This concentration can be attributed to the significant protection offered by guarantees from host governments and multilateral institutions. These sectors possess the capacity to generate substantial revenue through user fees, facilitating debt servicing and providing favorable returns on investment. Consequently, private investors and debt providers are drawn to participate in Africa's private sector investments, recognizing the potential for financial gains in these sectors (UNECA, 2020).

From 2014 to 2018, infrastructure funding in Africa primarily relied on international lenders and donors, except for the transport sector where governments played a major role. Private sector participation in infrastructure projects was limited, contributing only 7.5 percent of the funds. However, private investment in infrastructure was more substantial in Southern Africa, accounting for 24 percent of private infrastructure investment in Africa. In East, West, and Central Africa, private sector investment represented smaller proportions, approximately 9 percent and 6 percent respectively, indicating the need for increased private sector involvement in these regions (UNECA, 2020).

Bridging the infrastructure gap therefore requires the active participation of the national private sector. Engaging the private sector brings additional resources and expertise to meet the growing demand for infrastructure development, unlocking Africa's economic potential and fostering sustainable growth. Key considerations to effectively engage the national private sector in infrastructure financing are highlighted below.

1.3.2.1. Strengthening enabling frameworks

To attract the national private sector in infrastructure financing, policymakers must collaborate with relevant stakeholders to establish robust enabling frameworks. This involves implementing transparent and predictable regulatory frameworks, reducing bureaucracy, and ensuring the rule of law to instill investor confidence and facilitate private sector engagement. In addition, developing mechanisms to mitigate political, regulatory, and project-specific risks is crucial, and banks can play a pivotal role by providing guarantees, risk-sharing instruments, and creating conducive environments for dispute resolution (risk mitigation). Finally, strengthening institutions responsible for infrastructure project development and management, including regulatory bodies and public-private partnership units, enhances governance and improves project implementation capabilities.

1.3.2.2. Innovative financing mechanisms

African banks should explore innovative financing mechanisms to mobilize private sector investments in infrastructure. This includes leveraging blended finance models to de-risk projects and attract private sector capital by part-nering with development finance institutions and multilateral organizations. Furthermore, encouraging the establishment of infrastructure investment funds can mobilize long-term capital from domestic and international investors, such as pension funds and sovereign wealth funds. Sovereign wealth funds, deposit funds, and consignment funds can play a vital role in infrastructure financing by providing long-term, patient capital and mitigating the risks associated with infrastructure investments. Finally, promoting PPPs is also essential, as it creates opportunities for private sector involvement in infrastructure projects, ensuring clear allocation of risks and rewards between public and private entities (UNCTAD, 2021).

1.3.2.3. Leveraging digital banking and mining

The private sector in Africa, particularly telecommunication companies and the mining industry, harbor untapped wealth that can be harnessed for infra-structure development. In Côte d'Ivoire, for example, there are XOF5.1 billion in digital money accounts, serving as banks for those who do not have access to traditional banking services. This wealth is largely underutilized, with telecom companies gaining less revenue from traditional banking methods. A portion of these funds could be redirected to finance development projects. Innovative financing strategies, such as blended finance, can be employed to fund investments in the mining sector, where many African countries are rich but have limited benefits in terms of taxes. An example from Burkina Faso illustrates how a mining company's energy grid system, producing 65 MW, could be partially utilized to fulfil a 5 MW need for a solar panel project in the neighboring community, highlighting opportunities for collaboration. Revising mining codes and creating synergies between sectors like energy and mining can unlock additional resources. By strategically capturing this wealth from the informal sector through digital banking and innovative financing in mining, Africa can begin to close the infrastructure financing gap and enhance private sector involvement in sustainable growth.

1.3.2.3. Addressing sector-specific challenges

Recognizing sector-specific challenges, banks can take targeted actions to foster private sector participation. For example, in the energy sector, facilitating independent power production and renewable energy projects through policy incentives and regulatory support can attract private sector investments and address Africa's energy deficit. Similarly, enhancing transport infrastructure and promoting logistics hubs in the transport and logistics sector can improve connectivity, trade facilitation, and attract private investments. In the telecommunications and ICT sectors, encouraging private sector investments in expanding telecommunications networks and ICT infrastructure could promote digital inclusion and unlock economic opportunities.

1.3.2.4. Local content

Promoting local content in infrastructure projects enhances domestic participation, builds local capacity, creates economic opportunities for local companies and workforce and fosters long-term partnerships. Encouraging the transfer of technology, skills development, and capacity building can strengthen the local private sector's involvement in infrastructure financing and development.

1.4. Country case studies

This section presents how in Mauritius and South Africa, the private sector has contributed to each country's development agenda. It also highlights the constraints to the sector's development, the sector's experiences, and the role of public policy in enabling private actors to accelerate nation-building efforts. Where information, including data, is available, the section also sheds light on policy failures and how solutions were designed and implemented in specific contexts. The ultimate objective is that these countries' experiences and dynamics provide important lessons for peer learning and potential coordination/cooperation in policy alignment to harness the complementary role of the private sector.

1.4.1. Building self-sufficiency in development finance: The Mauritian experience

Mauritius, an African island nation in the southwest Indian Ocean, became an independent nation in 1968 after 253 years of colonization by the French (1715 to 1810) and the British (1810 to 1968). In the early years of independence, sugar production contributed to the bulk of the country's gross domestic product (GDP) and export earnings. The sugar industry was also the biggest employer in the country. Nonetheless, most vital economic indicators signaled a country that was heading towards an economic abyss. However, as a result of implementing appropriate growth models, Mauritius was able to graduate from the status of low-income country to that of upper middle-income in 1990 and to high income in 2019.[10] It also joined the league of Very High Human Development countries in 2020.[11] The availability of adequate and appropriate financing at the different stages of its development was determinant for its efforts to expand and diversify the economic base, secure a stable GDP growth path, create jobs, combat poverty, raise per capita income, and pull itself out of the low-income and middle-income traps.

This section discusses how Mauritius has achieved self-sufficiency in development finance. Here, self-sufficiency is defined as a country being able to meet its finance needs through its population and taxation. Mauritius achieved this by expanding its financial system, maintaining a relatively high ratio of tax revenue to GDP, and leveraging its export sector. The financial system and government revenue were key pathways, along with the export sector, for securing financing internally. This section explores the legacy of solid foundations in the financial system, identifies three phases and nine strategies for achieving self-sufficiency, focuses on how the country has maintained a relatively high ratio of tax revenue to GDP since the early 1970s, and discusses the government's use of leverage for revenue mobilization to widen the scope for raising development finance from within, and highlights the outcomes of the various strategies and policies to achieve self-sufficiency in development finance.

1.4.1.1. *Solid foundations for building self-sufficiency in development finance*

Mauritius started its financing from within journey with certain advantages that can be considered as positive stylized facts. The first of these is that the Mauritian economy depended on a surplus rather than subsistence agriculture model. The country initially relied on surplus agriculture, specifically sugar exports, to finance its development. However, the income generated from sugar was unequally distributed among just a few families. Taxation of the industry provided some funds, but not enough to meet the country's development finance

---

10 Based on the World Bank's ranking of countries by gross national income (GNI) per capita in current US$. In 2019, Mauritius' GNI per capita was estimated to be US$12 740 and above the high-income threshold. However, in 2020 due to the impact of the Covid-19 pandemic, the economy suffered a severe contraction of 14.9 percent and Mauritius' GNI per capita declined to US$10 230, while the high-income threshold was set at US$12 695.

11 According to the United Nations' Human Development Report 2021, Mauritius became a Very High Human Development nation in 2020 with a score of 0.804.

needs, so external financial aid and capital inflows were necessary during the early years of independence. Over time, the capital accumulated by sugar exporters became a significant source of funds for the country's economic expansion and diversification in the mid-1980s and 1990s.

The second stylized fact is that Mauritius has historically maintained high national savings, with an average gross domestic savings (GDS) to GDP ratio of around 24 percent from 1970 to 2007 (Figure 1). However, there has been a decline in the GDS/GDP ratio since 2008, reaching a low of 8.2 percent in 2020 and averaging 11.1 percent for the period 2008 to 2021. Merely looking at the level of domestic savings or its ratio to GDP or the savings-investment gap is insufficient to measure self-sufficiency in development finance. Instead, it is crucial to consider the financial system's ability to create money from bank deposits; while also recognizing that without access to foreign savings, the pool of loanable funds is constrained by the national savings rate.

Figure 1: Trends in total investment and total savings in 1968–2021, percent of GDP

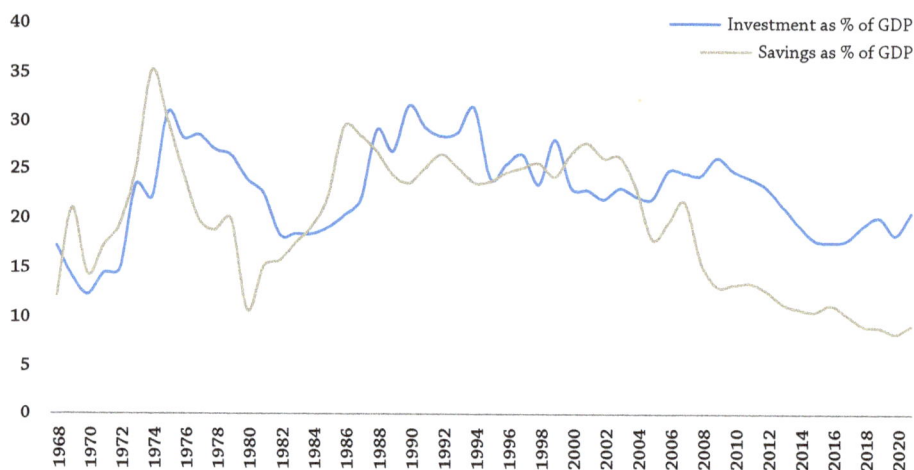

Source: Statistics Mauritius

The third stylized fact is that Mauritius already had a well-established banking sector and a monetized economy at the time of independence. The country had a long tradition of banking. Although the financial landscape seemed relatively underdeveloped in the late 1960s compared to the financing needs of the economy, there was a solid foundation to build upon.

1.4.1.2. Developing self-sufficiency in development finance in three phases

Mauritius' history of development financing from within can be divided into three distinct phases. The first phase spans from 1965 to 1990, followed by the second phase from 1991 to 2010, and the third phase from 2011 to the present. Over these periods, the government has pursued the goal of achieving self-sufficiency in financing through a sequence of nine strategies.

- The deepening of the banking sector.
- Expanding and diversifying the non-bank financial sector.
- Increasing the capacity of capital markets.
- Building up sovereign financial assets such as the National Pensions Fund and the foreign currency reserves of the central bank as potential sources of development finance.
- Enhancing government's capacity to raise tax revenues.
- Building up a network of parastatal companies and state-owned enterprises (SOEs) that, besides implementing and supporting government development policies, also generate revenue for government in the form of dividends and capital gains.
- Creating sovereign physical assets – real estate, land, and buildings – which can be used as a source of finance through asset monetization, if necessary.
- Making use of innovative and alternative ways of financing, including PPPs, various types of concession projects, and statutory corporate social responsibility.
- Using unconventional ways of financing in times of emergency such as transfers from the central bank to the consolidated fund.

Although it can be argued that the nine strategies mentioned above were implemented in the attributed sequence, it is important to note that there were instances of chronological overlapping throughout their execution.

i) First Phase: 1965–1990 - State dirigisme and building institutional capacity

During the first phase of Mauritius' development finance, the "state dirigisme" approach was extended to achieve self-sufficiency. This approach aimed to ensure inclusive access to finance for micro, small, and medium-sized enterprises, as well as align the financial system with broader development objectives rather than purely profit maximization. The Bank of Mauritius (BOM) was established in 1967 as the central bank, creating a framework for efficient resource allocation to finance development needs. The Development Bank Ltd was capitalized in 1970 to build up the development finance available for the agricultural and manufacturing sectors, and the State Bank of Mauritius (SBM Ltd) and State Insurance Company of Mauritius (SICOM Ltd) were established in 1973 and 1988 respectively. The National Pensions Fund and Stock Exchange of Mauritius (SEM Ltd) were also set up during this phase in 1976 and 1989 respectively.

Another distinct attribute of that first phase was the direct control measures that were imposed on bank lending to prioritize credit according to industrialization policies. This approach to credit control was to ensure that enough credit was extended to priority productive sectors while at the same time helping to curb inflationary pressures in the economy. These efforts resulted in significant improvement in banking system monetization and deepening, with substantial growth in deposits and widespread access to bank accounts by the 1980s. Specifically, the amount of time and savings deposits expanded more than twelvefold between 1967 and 1974, and by 1980 more than 80 percent of households had a bank account.

ii) Second Phase: 1991–2010 - Accelerating the development of the non-banking financial sector and capital markets

The second phase of Mauritius' development finance was characterized by an emphasis on expanding the non-bank financial sector and capital markets. In 1999, a cabinet minister was assigned the responsibility of developing the non-banking financial sector through the Ministry of Industry, Commerce, Corporate Affairs and Financial Services. This led to the creation of institutions such as the Mauritius Offshore Business Activities Authority (MOBAA), later replaced by the Financial Services Commission (FSC) in 2001, which became the regulator of non-banking financial services including stock exchange, insurance, pensions, and the global business sector. The establishment of the FSC filled a regulatory gap and brought coherence to financial policies.

Additionally, new institutions were established like the Port Louis Fund in 1997, the Financial Intelligence Unit in 2002, the Mauritius Post and Cooperative Bank in 2003, and the Financial Reporting Council in 2004. During this phase, there was a shift away from the "state dirigisme" approach, with steps taken to liberalize interest rates, remove credit ceilings, and suspend the Exchange Control Act. These reforms aimed to enhance efficiency in resource allocation by promoting market forces.

iii) Third Phase: 2011 to present - Managing a mature financial sector with a focus on inclusiveness, efficiency and internalization

This later phase of Mauritius' development finance is distinct from the previous phases in several ways. By the early 2010s, the financial sector had matured, characterized by a wide range of institutions, operators, and regulators. The empirical evidence indicated that development funding was sufficient. However, although there was adequate availability of development finance, a policy concern emerged regarding the accessibility of finance for specific business segments, especially micro, small, and medium-sized enterprises.

Phase III witnessed a significant emphasis on inclusiveness, which became a prominent aspect following the government's announcement of the Inclusive High Income Green Mauritius vision in 2019. In terms of financial institutions, Mauritius ranks 68th, 36th for financial depth, and 45th for efficiency, based on an IMF working paper which ranked 183 countries.[12] These rankings indicate the need for improvement in financial depth and efficiency while justifying policymakers' concerns regarding access to finance and inclusiveness. The strategy for inclusiveness focuses on providing finance access to diverse segments of the population, including entrepreneurs, students, and individuals across different income levels. Additionally, fiscal incentives and financing schemes are implemented in collaboration with commercial banks and financial institutions, including the DBM Ltd, MHC Ltd, and to a lesser extent, MauBank,[13] to facilitate access to finance.

Phase III also introduced a notable policy shift, focusing on the development of the equity financing sector, which stems from concerns about the high financial leverage of firms in the economy. The prevalence of high gearing ratios among enterprises poses significant risks (including financial, interest rate, operational risks) particularly during external shocks like the global recession and the Covid-19 pandemic. To address this, Mauritius emphasizes reducing financial leverage. Market capitalization of the Stock Exchange of Mauritius has increased over the past four decades, but it primarily reflects the value of existing stocks rather than new capital raised by listed companies (Figure 2). Additionally, market capitalization is concentrated in a small percentage of listed companies, and the stock market turnover ratio remains relatively low.

---

12 According to the same study, Mauritius does rather poorly in the country rankings on financial development, ranking 53rd on the Financial Development Index with a score of 0.389; 43rd on the Financial Institutions Index with a score of 0.562 and 61st on the Financial Markets Index with a score of 0.208.

13 In 2016, the Mauritius Post and Cooperative Bank changed its name to MauBank. The state now owns the second and third largest banks in the country, the SBM Ltd and the MauBank, respectively.

Figure 2: Stock Exchange of Mauritius, market capitalization, percent of GDP

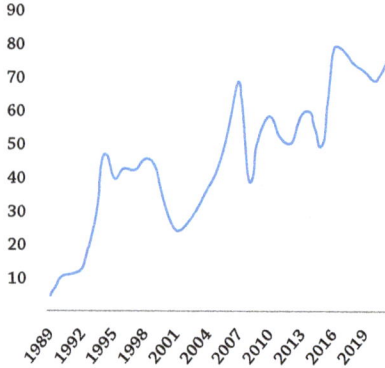

Figure 3: Excess cash holdings (MUR million)

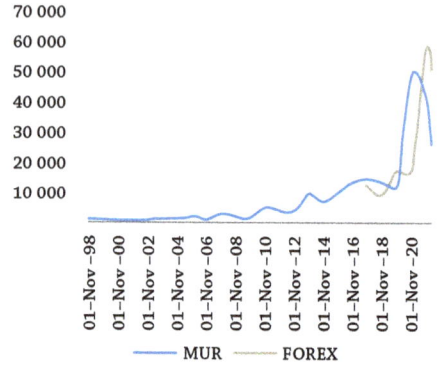

Source: Bank of Mauritius and Stock Exchange of Mauritius

Mauritian enterprises tend to prefer debt financing over equity financing due to three factors. First, excess liquidity in the banking system makes it convenient for enterprises to rely on bank loans (Figure 3). Second, the tax deductibility of interest paid on debt is an incentive. Lastly, enterprises in Mauritius generally have reservations about equity financing, particularly when it involves sharing ownership.

1.4.1.3. Optimizing government revenue to finance development

Fiscal policies in Mauritius have consistently aimed to optimize tax revenue since the early 1970s, maintaining a relatively high tax-to-GDP ratio of around 19 percent on average (in comparison to around 15 percent in Africa) (Figure 4).[14] Despite significant cuts in tax rates and the elimination of certain import taxes, the introduction of a sales tax in 1983 (later replaced by VAT), and the reduction of personal and corporate income tax rates,[15] tax revenue performances remained robust.

---

14 Data compiled by the World Bank at data.worldbank.org show average tax revenue to GDP ratios of 15 percent and 10.6 percent, respectively, for high income and upper middle-income countries in the year 2020. In that same year, the tax revenue to GDP ratio of Mauritius, which is in the upper middle-income group of countries, was 21.6 percent.
15 The top personal and corporate income tax rates were slashed to 35 percent from 70 percent, in 1985 and 1986, respectively. Subsequently, there were further reductions in income tax rates and in 2006, both personal and corporate income became subject to a flat tax rate of 15 percent.

Figure 4: Total tax revenue, percent of GDP

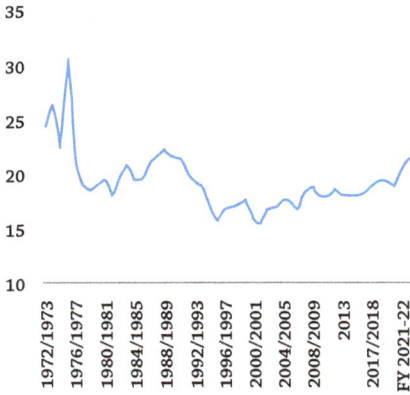

Figure 5: Revenue from sales tax and VAT, percent of GDP

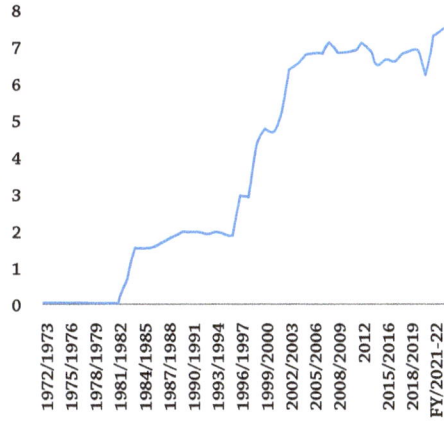

Source: Ministry of Finance, Economic Planning and Development, Government of Mauritius

Trade liberalization led to a decline in import taxes (Figure 6), compensated by the implementation of excise taxes on select goods and increased VAT revenue (Figure 5 and Figure 7). Tax administration reforms, including the establishment of the Mauritius Revenue Authority (MRA) in 2006, have further enhanced revenue collection, mitigated tax avoidance and evasion, and improved tax system efficiency and fairness. While the positive impact of these reforms is believed to be significant, concrete research confirming their outcomes is currently lacking.

Figure 6: Revenue from import duties as a ratio of GDP

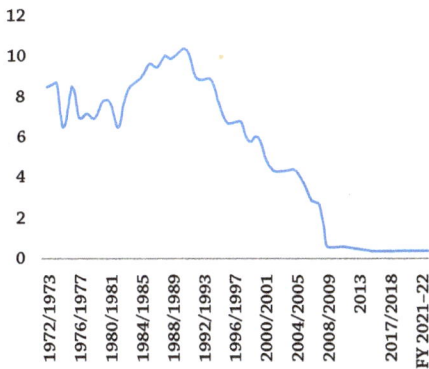

Figure 7: Revenue from excise duties as a ratio of GDP

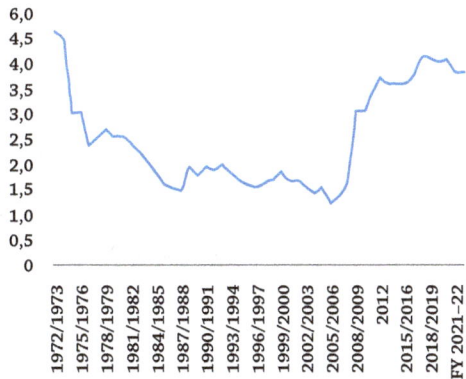

Source: Ministry of Finance, Economic Planning and Development, Government of Mauritius

1.4.1.4. Alternative financing for government

In recent years, during Phases II and III, the Mauritian Government has explored alternative financing methods to reduce borrowing and avoid debt accumulation. These methods include PPPs that are open to foreign investors, the imposition of statutory corporate social responsibility (CSR) on local companies, and the utilization of sovereign financial and physical assets through outright sales. While the government has considered selling physical assets like MauBank, the State Insurance Company, and the casinos (all state-owned), it has not yet devised a specific plan for asset monetization,[16] similar to ongoing efforts in India. Nonetheless, monetization presents a potential avenue for financing from within.

The government has also turned to unconventional domestic financing sources to support its budgetary needs. In 2019–2020, a substantial amount of money was transferred to the government from the Bank of Mauritius' Special Reserve Fund. This transfer was justified by utilizing idle assets to fund productive projects and address urgent financing requirements arising from the Covid-19 pandemic. As fiscal pressures mounted and debt metrics deteriorated, the Bank of Mauritius established the Mauritius Investment Company Ltd (MIC) in June 2020 to provide support to the economy. The creation of the MIC aligns with the central bank's mandate of promoting orderly and balanced economic development and ensuring the stability of the financial system. Although the move by the central bank has generated some controversy, it exemplifies the importance of building sovereign assets that can be readily utilized as a source of financing from within during times of need.

1.4.1.5. Outcomes of the 'financing from within' policies

Mauritius' financial depth as evidenced by the ratio of commercial bank assets to GDP, a crucial factor for achieving self-sufficiency in development finance, improved significantly in recent decades (Figure 8). This ratio surged from 30 percent of GDP to 67 percent during Phase I, further increasing to 352 percent by the end of Phase II, and reaching 435 percent in 2021. Figure 9 illustrates the upward trajectory of credit to the private sector as a percentage of GDP. Credit to the private sector climbed from 19 percent of GDP to 33 percent in Phase I, then rose to 68 percent by the conclusion of Phase II, and further escalated to 85 percent in the most recent year of Phase III (Figure 9).

---

16 The Union Government announced an asset monetization plan in August 2021 wherein brownfield or existing public assets worth MUR6 trillion (or US$135.9 million) were to be monetized by leasing them out to private sector partners for fixed terms with the aim of utlilizing the proceeds for capital expenditure towards new infrastructure.

The significant increase in the size of broad money[17] relative to the country's GDP also illustrates the deepening of the financial sector (Figure 10).

Figure 8: Financial assets, percent of GDP

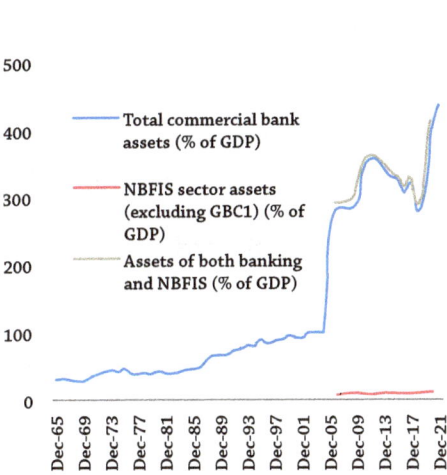

Total commercial bank assets (% of GDP)

NBFIS sector assets (excluding GBC1) (% of GDP)

Assets of both banking and NBFIS (% of GDP)

Figure 9: Total credit to the private sector, percent of GDP

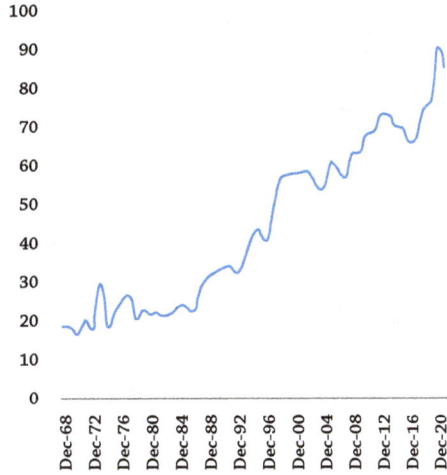

Figure 10: Ratio of broad money to GDP

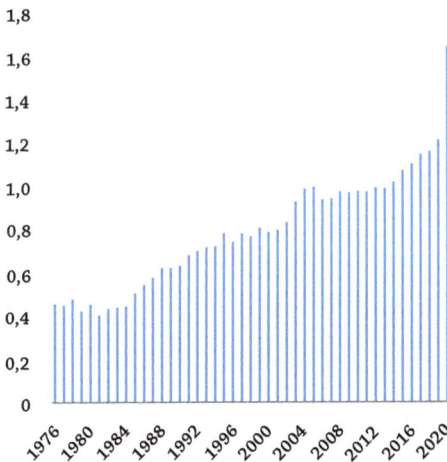

Figure 11: Number of companies and securities listed on the SEM

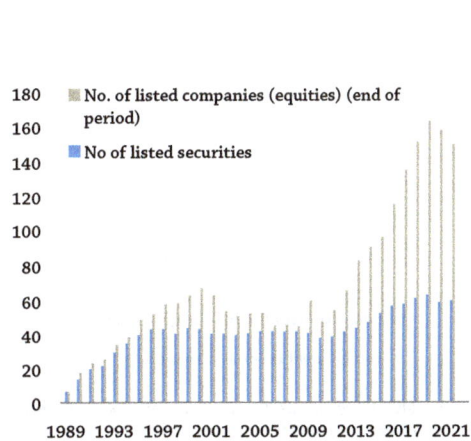

No. of listed companies (equities) (end of period)

No of listed securities

Source: Bank of Mauritius; Stock Exchange of Mauritius; World Development Indicators

---

17 Broad money excludes deposits of global businesses.

Two categories of shares are listed on the stock market in Mauritius (Figure 11), including the shares traded on the official market, which is the Stock Exchange of Mauritius (SEM) and those listed on the Development and Enterprise Market (DEM) for companies that have to meet less stringent listing requirements. However, the rising value of market capitalization on the SEM is not primarily due to equity financing. The stock market has not fulfilled its expected role in contributing to internal financing, although it holds potential for firms to raise capital. On the other hand, the excess liquidity in the banking sector suggests success in generating development finance from within (Figure 3). Despite this, there is still unmet demand for loans from private enterprises, especially small and medium-sized enterprises, emphasizing the need for inclusiveness in Phase III of the financial sector.

Examining the composition of the government's debt portfolio, including both external and domestic sources, provides additional insight into the attainment of self-sufficiency in development finance. It is important to note that achieving self-sufficiency does not imply that the government's debt portfolio will solely consist of domestic borrowing.

Figure 12: Domestic and external sources of government financing

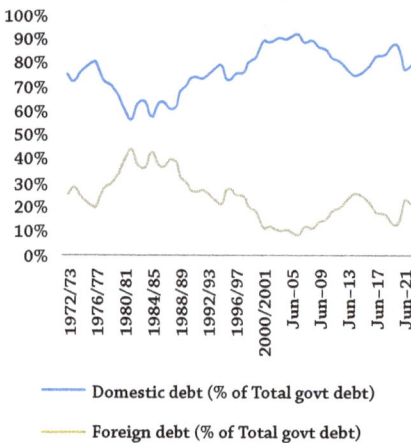

Domestic debt (% of Total govt debt)

Foreign debt (% of Total govt debt)

Figure 13: Debt service ratio, percent of exports

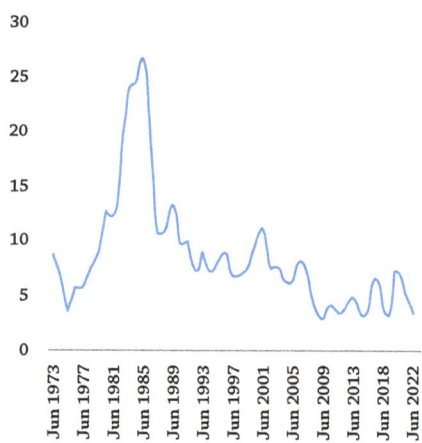

Source: Ministry of Finance, Economic Planning and Development
Note: (i) All data featured in Figures 12 and 13 are from the end of the fiscal year. The different dates in both graphs reflect changes in the definition of the fiscal year. (ii) The debt service ratio measures interest and capital repayment as a percentage of total export earnings.

Achieving self-sufficiency in development finance provides a government with greater flexibility in determining the balance between domestic and external debt. Mauritius, benefiting from enhanced capacity to mobilize funds internally, has been able to repay costly foreign borrowings. In the past two decades, the country's external debt averaged 16 percent of GDP, compared to 27.7 percent in the preceding period. By relying on the domestic market to meet its financing needs, Mauritius has avoided borrowing from international markets since 1995, reducing costs and risks associated with external debt. The debt-service ratio has remained below 10 percent since 1990, considered safe for a developing nation (Figure 13). Most foreign debts are owed to development agencies and bilateral partners, offering concessional rates and favorable terms.

However, one major weakness in the financial structure of Mauritius is the thinness of its bond market, dominated by government and central bank issuances. Efforts to develop the secondary bond market have faced challenges due to the prevailing buy-and-hold strategy among bond purchasers.

1.4.2. Well-developed financial markets but low investment rates: The South African paradox

South Africa presents an interesting case study, having one of the most developed financial markets in the world, but low rates of fixed capital formation. For example, the equity market, dominated by the Johannesburg Stock Exchange, is deep and liquid, with a market capitalization/GDP[18] ratio of over 300 percent, far exceeding that of other emerging markets but also advanced economies such as the United States and Republic of Korea.

The country's fixed investment to GDP ratio is at a historical low (12.5 percent of GDP), and for some time, has tended to be on the lower end for an emerging market. The National Development Plan sets a long-term target for fixed investment at 30 percent of GDP. To address this challenge, in April 2018, President Ramaphosa announced an investment mobilization drive for his incoming administration, setting a target for investment of US$100 billion (ZAR1.2 trillion) over 5 years.[19] The establishment of an investment drive led by the President has put investment mobilization at the center of government policy development and implementation. Though there is no explicit target for domestic investment versus foreign direct investment, a high proportion of the investment has been by local firms. Yet despite the apparent success of this drive, with over 95 percent of new deals recorded, the investment to GDP ratio has deteriorated. This reflects

---

18 Stocks listed multiplied by share prices.
19 When the announcement was made, South Africa was emerging from a decade of state capture, low business confidence, and weak investor sentiment. Few anticipated the subsequent global pandemic. Despite these challenges, five years later, the investment target has not only been met but exceeded by 26%. The President proudly announced at the recent South Africa Investment Conference (SAIC) that ZAR1.51 trillion in investment pledges had been secured, surpassing the initial ZAR1.2 trillion goal. Buoyed by this success, a new target of ZAR2 trillion in investments over the next five years was set (South African High Commission Canada, 2023).

the low degree of business confidence as tracked by various surveys, the effects of Covid-19 containment measures and the stagnation of investment in key sectors of the economy, such as mining.

Figure 14: Market capitalization as a percent of GDP

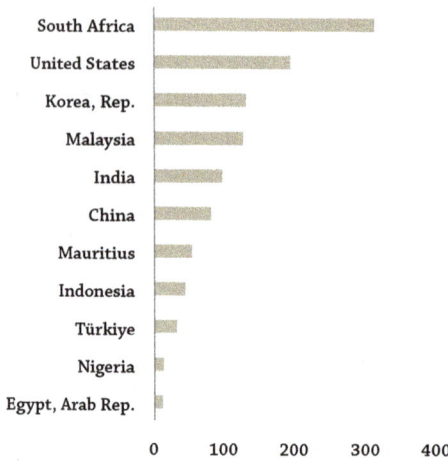

Figure 15: Gross-fixed capital formation, private sector (percent of GDP) in a few countries

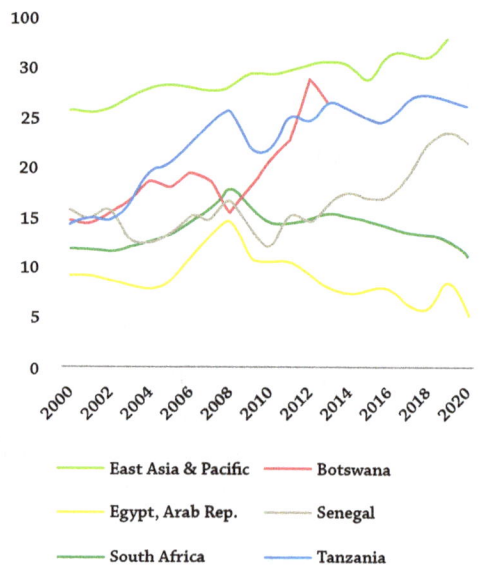

Source: World Development Indicators

The role of the private sector in bridging this gap is well acknowledged by policymakers. As Finance Minister Enoch Gondongwana argued:

> Between 2010 and 2020, public-sector capital investment averaged 5.8 percent of GDP, while private capital investment averaged 11.2 percent of GDP. Total investment is well below the National Development Plan target of 30 percent – and has been declining since 2015. To reach this target, public-sector investment would need to grow from 3.9 percent of GDP in 2020 to 10 percent of GDP by 2030, while private-sector investment in infrastructure would need to grow from 9.8 percent of GDP in 2020 to 20 percent in 2030.[20]

---

20 Speech by the Minister of Finance, Mr Enoch Godongwana, at the Consulting Engineers South Africa Infrastructure Indaba, on August 18th, 2022, https://www.gov.za/news/speeches/minister-enoch-godongwana-consulting-engineers-south-africa-infrastructure-indaba-18.

The significance of the private sector in capital formation in South Africa is lower than in other African countries such as Botswana, Tanzania, and Senegal, which have all seen higher and growing proportion of relative private sector capital formation. In the East Asia and Pacific regions, the private sector plays a far more prominent role in capital formation, at rates over 30 percent of GDP (Figure 15).

Domestic business sentiment is anecdotally worse than foreign investor confidence. Structural reforms have been the key demand from local business. These include energy security, improving the efficiency of ports and rail and local government service provision (water, permits). These are similar to constraints identified in other African markets. Policy deadlocks in various areas have also undermined business confidence including road tolling, land reform, spectrum allocation and digital migration (resolved), energy sector reform (work in progress).

1.4.2.1. Improving the role of the private sector in financing infrastructure

The Addis Ababa Action Agenda (AAAA) acknowledges that

> ... impediments to private investment in infrastructure exist on both the demand and supply side. Insufficient investment is due in part to inadequate infrastructure plans and an insufficient number of well-prepared investable projects, along with private sector incentive structures that are not necessarily appropriate for investing in many long-term projects, and risk perceptions of investors.[21]

The AAAA commits to putting in place international support mechanisms to help countries realize their infrastructure goals. It also calls on institutional investors such as pension funds to allocate a greater percentage to infrastructure.

In South Africa, there is a substantial stock of funds amounting to ZAR14.2 trillion, with inflows of approximately ZAR170 billion per year in 2019 (Figure 16). The financial sector indirectly supports infrastructure development through investments in sovereign and state-owned enterprise (SOE) bonds, totaling around ZAR1 trillion. Additionally, the sector directly contributes to infrastructure financing at an estimated 1.5 percent, slightly higher than the OECD average of 1.3 percent. The top six banks in the country hold government securities, which accounted for over 12 percent of their assets as of January 2021.

There has been a notable rise in the emergence of private sector impact finance and environmental, social, and governance (ESG) funds. These funds have a specific mandate to invest in infrastructure, climate change initiatives,

---

21 United Nations (2015)

and public goods. However, questions have been raised regarding whether these initiatives mobilize additional funds for public goods and if they represent a distinct approach to financing. One aspect of scrutiny revolves around the expectations of returns from such investments and whether they genuinely differ from traditional investment models.

Figure 16: South Africa's stock of funds in 2019 (ZAR)

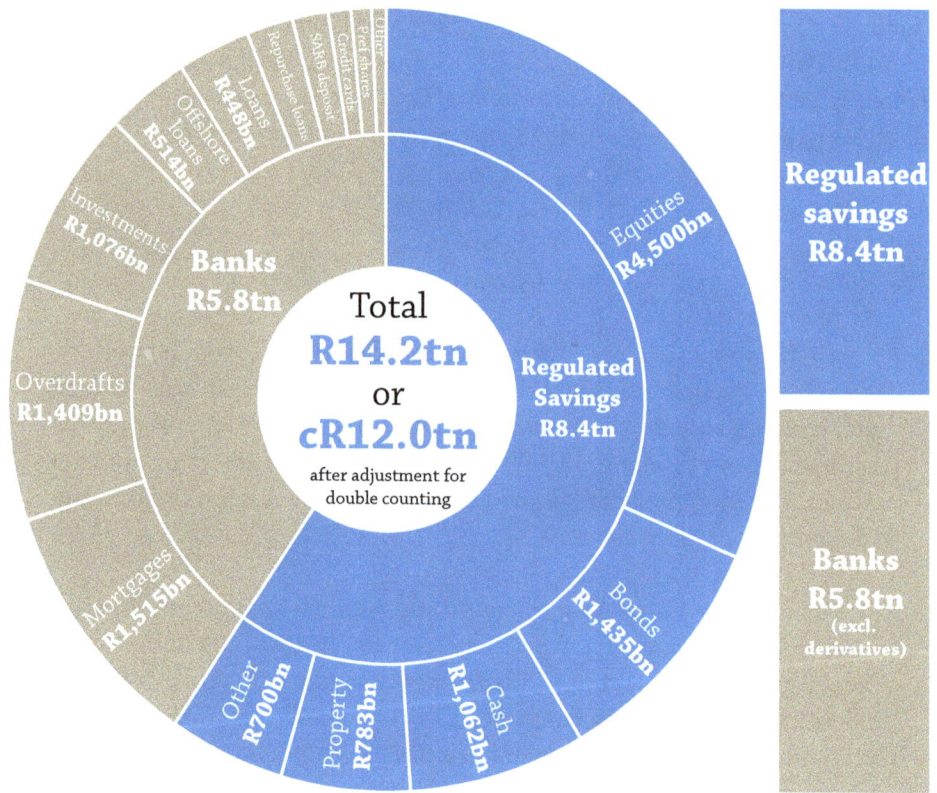

Source: IMF Financial Sector Stability Assessment 2022, B4SA

One of the challenges South Africa faces is the availability of fundable projects to match the existing pool of funds ("project pipeline challenge"). To address this issue, the Budget Facility for Infrastructure was introduced in 2017. This mechanism aims to enhance project preparation and improve the pipeline of viable projects. In parallel, the Infrastructure Fund was established in South Africa, conceptualized as a blended finance vehicle that combines government budgetary allocation of ZAR100 billion over ten years with the aim of attracting significant private finance. The Infrastructure Fund is hosted within the Development Bank of Southern Africa, acting as a platform to bring in private investment and play a significant role in the infrastructure ecosystem. Furthermore, regulatory changes have been implemented to target infrastructure development, including modifications to pension fund regulations that allow for the inclusion of alternative assets. These initiatives demonstrate the efforts made in South Africa to stimulate infrastructure investment, bridge the financing gap, and create an environment conducive to attracting private sector participation in infrastructure projects.

1.4.2.2. Tapping into private pension funds

Enabling private sector retirement funds to increase investment in infrastructure has been high on the agenda. The tendency is towards shaping the incentives and the enabling environment to favor private sector involvement in infrastructure, as opposed to a prescriptive approach. The National Treasury has amended a key regulation of the Pension Funds Act (Regulation 28) to raise the asset threshold for infrastructure investment by pension funds. The regulation does not prescribe which assets a pension fund should choose, rather it is a long-standing regulatory directive that places maxima on the asset types that a pension fund may invest in. This is to protect members from concentration risk and asset classes perceived to be high risk. As of January 2023, the amendment introduces a definition of infrastructure and sets a limit of 45 percent for infrastructure assets. This builds on the unlisted allowance of 35 percent that prevails. The amendment also separates the limit between hedge funds and private equity, with the maximum for private equity lifted to 15 percent from 10 percent.

1.4.2.3. Public-private partnerships

According to the 2022 Budget Review:

> The value of PPPs has steadily declined in recent years, from an estimated ZAR 10.7 billion in 2011/12 to ZAR 5.6 billion in 2019/20. This is partly due to onerous approval processes, especially for small projects, and poor capacity of departments to estimate risk-sharing with the private sector. At the same time, lack of clarity regarding the user-pays principle affects

the cost of state guarantees. A PPP review concluded by the National Treasury in September 2021 emphasized the need to simplify approval and compliance requirements, and reform the policy framework to assess and prioritize PPPs. This is expected to encourage private-sector financing solutions. The review recommends that government create a PPP Centre of excellence, and that an expedited approval process be considered for projects below ZAR 1 billion in value. The National Treasury aims to implement these reforms over the next 24 months.

Overall, the seeming paradox of South Africa's investment climate can be understood through the lens of its domestic savings rates. Gross domestic savings in South Africa are relatively low, primarily driven by the corporate sector's savings. Both the household and public sectors contribute minimally to positive savings, resulting in gross domestic savings amounting to only about 17 percent of GDP on average between 2020 and 2023.[22] The lack of sufficient domestic savings discourages private investment, despite innovations aimed at stimulating PPPs through infrastructure funds. Additionally, issues related to infrastructure and governance, further deter private investment. Consequently, the scarcity of savings limits the potential for increased capital investment, posing a significant challenge to sustainable economic growth and development in South Africa.

1.4.3. Financial sector development: The way forward

1.4.3.1. Mobilization of financing and bank contribution

In African economies, many sectors, such as agriculture, still struggle with mobilizing sufficient and adequate financing, decades after the Monterrey Conference landmark agreements.[23] The commitments were articulated around six components: domestic resource mobilization; the mobilization of international resources, including FDI; trade as an engine for development; international cooperation; debt; systemic linkages between finance and previous components. However, there are several going reflections and initiatives to diversify the sources of financing, optimize the structure of financing by source and attract more external financing.

i) Afrexim Bank – PAPSS

---

22 Data from World Development Indicators.
23 The Monterrey Conference is the first United Nations summit to address key financial issues pertaining to global development (United Nations, 2002).

The African Export-Import, or Afrexim, Bank holds a prominent position as the leading trade finance institution in Africa, dedicated to fostering the expansion, diversification, and overall development of African trade. At the core of its mission is the establishment of a unified payment infrastructure that effectively overcomes exchange barriers and facilitates instant fund transfers. One of the notable initiatives pioneered by Afrexim Bank is the Pan-African Payment and Settlement System (PAPSS). This innovative system aims to streamline and secure monetary transactions across African borders, minimizing associated risks and actively contributing to the financial integration of regional economies. Through collaboration with African central banks, PAPSS provides a reliable payment and settlement service accessible to commercial banks, payment service providers, and fintech companies throughout the continent. By increasing the volume of cross-border payments, this initiative significantly advances the development of the financial sector in African countries, fostering economic growth and enhancing financial connectivity across the region.

ii) Capital market enhancement

Africa currently boasts 29 stock exchanges, collectively representing a market capitalization that accounts for nearly 60 percent of the continent's GDP. However, it is evident that stock exchanges alone do not make a sufficient contribution to Africa's overall development. Nonetheless, initial public offerings (IPOs) present notable advantages, including the potential for raising capital to fuel growth, providing liquidity to shareholders, and enhancing the visibility and credibility of listed companies.

To foster the development of the financial sector in Africa, several key factors come into play. These include the admission of new companies to the stock exchange, the dissemination of financial information and investor education, the attraction of new investors, and the deepening of market activity. It is through these elements that the stock exchange can facilitate the formation of a virtuous circle to which the emergence of a new category of investors made up of an educated and informed middle class would contribute.

iii) Call for guarantee funds

A guarantee fund is intended to compensate for possible losses in credit operations due to the default of borrowers. On a continent where there is a proliferation of small businesses seeking financing, the mechanism would ease the connection between existing financial channels and specific types of customers, such as micro-enterprises, with profiles and needs. The development of guarantee funds would encourage microfinance institutions, as well as commercial banks, to lend directly to micro-enterprises. The reduction of losses through this insurance mechanism, borne by the borrower, leads to an increase in the profitability of loans or a reduction in their costs.

1.4.3.2. How to attract the domestic private sector?

A set of reforms must be put in place in African countries to motivate private sector financing of infrastructure.

Table 3. Regulatory reforms to enable private sector financing of infrastructure

Area of reform	Main action	Expected impact
Private sector	Mobilize local financial markets that are not used to directly financing infrastructure projects but wish to exploit stable long-term investment opportunities.	Reduction of exchange rate risks, economic development and increase in the overall level of investment
	Maximizing fiscal space by leveraging private sector balance sheet capacity and risk sharing	
	Distribution of financial obligations	Easing fiscal pressures on state-owned enterprises
	Improving access to foreign capital and financial markets	Increased investment
	Tariff mechanisms to recover costs and adapt to changing circumstances	Improving the solvency of companies
	Development of strong agreements	Minimizing political and institutional risks
	Transparent competitive tenders	Control costs and reduce opportunities for corruption
	Public disclosure of tender and award conditions	
	Public-private dialogue	Improving the investment and business climate

Conclusion

This chapter examines the private sector in Africa and proposes strategies that could be put in place not only to improve the contribution of African banks, institutional investors, and other private sector actors to development financing, but also, and above all, to involve the domestic private sector in infrastructure financing.

To accelerate the contribution of banks and institutional investors to development financing in Africa, several key strategies can be implemented. Strengthening financial systems through improved regulations and supervision, promoting financial inclusion through innovative fintech solutions, and developing sustainable financial instruments aligned with environmental and social objectives are crucial steps. Facilitating public-private partnerships, strengthening governance and risk management frameworks, and investing in capacity-building and knowledge-sharing initiatives are also essential. By implementing these measures, Africa can unlock the potential of its financial sector and drive sustainable and inclusive development on the continent.

To address Africa's infrastructure gap, the present circumstances necessitate the exploration of diverse funding sources. Among these sources, the national private sector plays a crucial role. To achieve this, strengthening enabling frameworks through policy and regulatory reforms, risk mitigation mechanisms, and institutional capacity building is crucial. Innovative financing mechanisms like blended finance, infrastructure investment funds, and public-private partnerships can mobilize private sector investments. Addressing sector-specific challenges in energy, transport, and telecommunications sectors further enhances private sector participation. By implementing these strategies, African countries can create an attractive investment climate, driving sustainable infrastructure development and economic growth on the continent.

References

Africa CEO Forum (2014) *The private sector, driving force of Africa's growth*. Available at: https://www2.deloitte.com/content/dam/Deloitte/fpc/Documents/nous-connaitre/deloitte-afrique-francophone/deloitte_africa-ceo-forum-the-private-sector-driving-force.pdf

African Development Bank (AfDB) and Development Centre of the Organisation for Economic Co-operation and Development (OECD) (2010) *African economic outlook 2010*. OECD, African Development Bank and United Nations Economic Commission for Africa. Paris: OECD. Available at: https://www.oecd-ilibrary.org/development/african-economic-outlook-2010_aeo-2010-en

AfDB (2011) *African development report 2011: The role of the private sector in Africa's economic development*. Abidjan, Côte d'Ivoire: African Development Bank.

African Infrastructure Investment Managers (AIIM) (2017) *Role of the private sector in the infrastructure spending gap*. Available at: https://aiimafrica.com/media/media-centre/role-of-the-private-sector-in-the-infrastructure-spending-gap/

African Peer Review Mechanism (APRM) and United Nations Economic Commission for Africa (UNECA) (2023) *Africa sovereign credit rating review: 2023 Mid-year outlook*. 7th edn. Addis Ababa: UN Economic Commission for Africa (UNECA) and the African Peer Review Mechanism (APRM). Available at: https://repository.uneca.org/bitstream/handle/10855/49850/b12035440.pdf?sequence=1&isAllowed=y

Gorecki, I. (2020) 'Kenya's Standard Gauge Railway: The promise and risks of rail megaprojects,' *Africa Up Close*, 24 September. Available at: https://www.wilsoncenter.org/blog-post/kenyas-standard-gauge-railway-the-promise-and-risks-of-rail-megaprojects

International Finance Corporation (IFC) (2018) *The unseen sector: A report on the MSME opportunity in South Africa*. Washington, DC: International Finance Corporation (IFC), World Bank Group. Available at: https://documents1.worldbank.org/curated/en/710801548830275900/pdf/134151-WP-ZA-Unseen-Sector-MSME-Opportunity-South-Africa-PUBLIC.pdf

International Labour Organization (ILO) (2018) *Women and men in the informal economy: A statistical picture.* 3rd edn. Geneva: International Labour Organization. Available at: https://www.ilo.org/sites/default/files/wcmsp5/groups/public/@dgreports/@dcomm/documents/publication/wcms_626831.pdf

International Labour Organization (ILO) (2020) *The impact of the COVID-19 on the informal economy in Africa and the related policy responses.* Geneva: International Labour Organization. Available at: https://www.ilo.org/wcmsp5/groups/public/---africa/---ro-abidjan/documents/briefingnote/wcms_741864.pdf

International Monetary Fund (IMF) (2021) *Private finance for development: Wishful thinking or thinking out of the box?* Washington, DC: IMF, The African Department. Available at: https://www.imf.org/en/Publications/Departmental-Papers-Policy-Papers/Issues/2021/05/14/Private-Finance-for-Development-50157

International Social Security Association (2021) *Africa 2021. Priorities for social security: Trends, challenges and solutions.* Geneva: ISSA. Available at: https://www.issa.int/sites/default/files/documents/2021-09/2-Four%20Priorities%20Africa%20WEB.pdf

Nishio, A. (2019) 'The private sector can be a powerful partner in West Africa and the Sahel,' *World Bank Blogs,* 25 September. Available at: https://blogs.worldbank.org/voices/private-sector-can-be-powerful-partner-west-africa-and-sahel

Patel, O. (2022) 'Projects like Kenya's Standard Gauge Railway can unlock development,' *The Conversation,* 11 April. Available at: https://theconversation.com/projects-like-kenyas-standard-gauge-railway-can-unlock-development-177464

Sena, K. (2023) *The drivers of investment and savings rates: An exploratory note.* UNCTAD. Available at: https://unctad.org/system/files/official-document/diaeia2023d3a5_en.pdf

South African High Commission Canada (2023) 'South Africa's investment target surpasses expectations', 24 April. Available at: http://www.southafrica-canada.ca/2023/04/24/investment-target-surpasses/

United Nations (2002) *Monterrey Consensus of the international conference on financing for development, Monterrey, Mexico.* New York: United Nations. Avaiable at: https://www.un.org/esa/ffd/overview/monterrey-conference.html.

United Nations (2015) *Addis Ababa Action Agenda of the third international conference on financing development.* Addis Ababa Action Agenda: Addis Ababa, Ethiopia. Available at: https://sustainabledevelopment.un.org/content/documents/ 2051AAAA_Outcome.pdf.

United Nations Conference on Trade and Development (UNCTAD) (2015) *Strengthening the private sector to boost continental trade and integration in Africa.* UNCTAD Policy Brief No. 33. Geneva: UNCTAD. Available at: https://unctad.org/system/files/official-document/presspb2015d5_en.pdf

UNCTAD (2021) *Private sector engagement in LDCs: Challenges and gaps.* Geneva: UNCTAD. Available at: https://unctad.org/system/files/non-official-document/ldcr2019_bn_1_en.pdf

United Nations Economic Commission for Africa (UNECA) (2019) *Economic report on Africa 2019: Fiscal policy for financing sustainable development in Africa.* Addis Ababa: United Nations Economic Commission for Africa.

UNECA (2020) *Economic report on Africa 2020: Innovative finance for private sector development in Africa.* Addis Ababa: UNECA. Available at: https://www.uneca.org/sites/default/files/fullpublicationfiles/ERA_2020_mobile_20201213.pdf

UNECA (2023) 'Private sector urged to "own and drive" Africa's continental free trade,' *Africa Renewal,* 26 January. Available at: https://www.un.org/africarenewal/magazine/january-2023/private-sector-urged-%E2%80%9Cown-and-drive%E2%80%9D-africa%E2%80%99s-continental-free-trade

World Bank (2021) *The global findex database 2021: Financial inclusion, digital payments, and resilience in the age of COVID-19.* Washington, DC: World Bank Group.

Yieke, L. (2023) 'New era of high interest rates puts Africa in tough spot,' *African Business,* 17 October. Available at: https://african.business/2023/10/trade-investment/new-era-of-high-interest-rates-puts-africa-in-tough-spot

CHAPTER 2

Digital Technologies and Taxation

2.1. Introduction

Digitalization continues to transform economies around the world through the emergence of new business models and ways of working. Digital technologies provide new ways for buyers and sellers to interact both locally and globally and trigger the expansion of e-commerce. Limitations to in-person interactions due to Covid-19 have further accelerated the use of information and communications technologies (ICT). One of the biggest African e-commerce platforms, Jumia, saw an increase of over 50 percent in the volume of transactions during the first six months of 2020, compared with the same period in 2019 (UN, 2021).

The digital revolution is a key enabler of sustainable development. Digital transformation is a driving force for innovative, inclusive, and sustainable growth. Innovations and digitalization are stimulating job creation and contributing to addressing poverty, reducing inequality, facilitating the delivery of goods and services, and contributing to the achievement of Agenda 2063 and the sustainable development goals.[24] Information technology can greatly enhance tax mobilization in developing countries. Utilizing advanced tools and systems, these countries can increase tax revenue, create fiscal space, and address infrastructure gaps, thereby bolstering economic development. Digitizing tax payments and related processes in emerging and developing countries can raise an additional US$300 billion in government revenues annually (Better Than Cash Alliance, 2020).

In recent decades, there has been a trend towards the modernization of customs and tax administration across Africa through the adoption of electronic filing and tax payment systems. According to the World Bank Group GovTech data, in 2022, electronic filing was available for tax and/or customs declarations in 23 SSA countries out of 48, and implementation was in progress in six other countries. Also, electronic tax payment was available in 19 SSA countries. Electronic filing and payment refers to digital services that allow taxpayers to (i) file their taxes electronically (together with a range of other

---

24 The African Union's (2019) Digital Transformation Strategy for Africa 2020–2030.

tax-related activities, such as attaching annexures, claiming for refunds, making appeals, updating their personal details, getting assistance online, checking their filing histories, etc.), usually through a web portal to which they have access or through similar phone applications; (ii) to perform payments of tax liabilities online, by means of digital platforms (mobile money, credit card or similar electronic transfers) which efficiently connect the revenue authority, private banks or digital financial service providers, and the central bank (Okunogbe and Santoro, 2022).

Digital technology adoption in tax administration has several beneficial effects, including an increase in tax performance through strengthening the capacity of tax administrations to identify tax bases and facilitating the tracking of illegal operations. Digitalization reduces direct interaction between taxpayers and tax officers, thus reducing opportunities for corruption and rent-seeking activities and fostering transparency. Since the introduction of electronic invoicing in Rwanda in 2013, fraudulent value-added tax (VAT) claims have been reduced by 25–35 percent. The World Customs Organization's Arusha Declaration Concerning Good Governance and Integrity in Customs (1993, revised in 2003) highlights the relevance of the computerization of customs functions as a key pillar in reducing corruption and increasing levels of accountability. Modernization of customs and tax systems improves the efficiency of tax collection through cost and time saving in tax collection and tax payment. Thus, the use of digital tools leads to an increase in tax compliance by reducing the compliance burden on taxpayers (Colin *et al.*, 2015) and making it easy for them to obtain information and fulfil their tax obligations. In Guinea, the tax revenues on international trade increased by 151.6 percent 8 months after the technology adoption. Furthermore, charging tax on digital transactions offers a promising way to increase tax revenue and target tax avoidance. Taxation of the digital economy in Africa through new direct digital service taxes or broadened existing indirect taxes could lead to consequent revenue gains, especially as the share of the African population making online purchases is expected to increase to 40 percent in 2025, compared with 13 percent in 2017.[25] Since the implementation of its cross-border VAT on electronic services in 2014, South Africa has raised about US$929 million (OECD, 2021a).

While offering opportunities to broaden the tax base and making tax revenue collection more efficient, digitalization poses significant tax challenges. The growth of the digital economy provides many challenges to direct tax systems through the rise of new ways of working and types of assets, facilitating the mobility of taxpayers and raising the question of how taxing rights on income

---

25 This figure is from the OECD/WBG/ATAF 2023 VAT Toolkit for Africa: https://www.oecd.org/tax/consumption/vat-digital-toolkitfor-africa.htm

generated from cross-border activities should be allocated among jurisdictions. Like tax systems in other regions, African tax systems were not designed for cryptocurrencies. VAT challenges of digital trade lie in the ability of businesses to conduct activities within a jurisdiction without having a physical activity or having a physical presence in that jurisdiction, making tax collection difficult under traditional procedures. Thus, the lack of adequate legislation for taxing digital services limits countries' ability to leverage e-commerce opportunities.

Moreover, inadequate infrastructure and connectivity and the low digital skill level of users (taxpayers and tax officials) undermine the potential gains from the use of new technology in Africa. The region displays the largest usage gap of digital infrastructure in the world. Although 84 percent of country populations averaged across sub-Saharan Africa had at least some level of 3G mobile internet availability and 63 percent had some level of 4G mobile internet services, only 22 percent used mobile internet services as of the end of 2021 (Begazo et al., 2023). Also, significant disparities remain within countries, with a usage gap between less educated and better educated people, and taxpayers living in rural areas compared with those living in urban areas. In addition, as displayed in the 2022 GSMA report on the mobile gender gap, SSA has among the widest gender gaps in mobile internet use in the world, with over 190 million women not using mobile internet services, a 37 percent gender gap. Thus, significant efforts are needed to address these digital divides and harness the potential of the new technology in Africa. International cooperation through tax negotiations and information, knowledge and experience sharing also plays a significant role in building adequate and innovative solutions to meet these challenges.

This chapter focuses on how African countries could unlock the potential of new technology to increase governments' domestic revenue mobilization (DRM) performance through both digitalization of tax administration and taxation of the digital economy.

The chapter first looks closely at the opportunities that digitalization provides for improving DRM to support the SDGs (section 2). Then, it reviews the environmental constraints to reaping digital dividends in Africa, the tax challenges associated with digitalization and the multilateral efforts to address these challenges (section 3). Illustrative country case studies focused on the Democratic Republic of Congo, Guinea and Rwanda are presented (section 4). The chapter also aims to provide policymakers with key lessons for successful ICT reforms in tax administration learned from the experiences of African and international peers on how to harness digital technologies to improve tax compliance and performance (section 5). The chapter ends by considering how tax authorities can improve their practices to reach higher levels of digitalization, or digital maturity, to fully benefit from the digital revolution (section 6); and section 7 concludes.

2.2. Harnessing digitalization to enhance domestic resource mobilization

Digitalization is the process of spreading general-purpose technology.[26] The use of digital technologies creates opportunities for governments to mobilize more revenue, reduce the compliance burden on taxpayers, make tax collection more effective, modernize tax codes, and improve the design of tax systems. It also provides opportunities for tax administrations to protect their tax bases and tackle cross-broader tax evasion more effectively through increased international cooperation and the exchange of information. The potential of modernizing tax systems to improve tax performance is also supported by empirical evidence (Bate, 2021; Brun *et al.*, 2020; Kochanova, Hasnain and Larson, 2020; Bellon *et al.*, 2022; Koyuncu, Yilmaz and Ünver, 2016). On average, tax performance, business environment rating and efficiency of revenue mobilization rating were higher in SSA countries where e-filing for tax and/or customs declarations were available or in implementation in 2020, compared with the average for SSA countries where customs and tax administration were not modernized (Figure 17). Also, the average annual time to comply with tax law measures was longer (more than 200 hours) in countries with traditional tax-filing systems.[27]

Figure 17: Efficiency of tax systems in African countries*

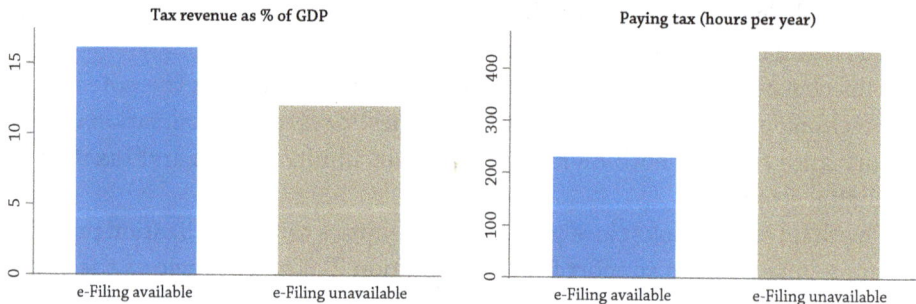

26 European Commission (2014). General-purpose technology or GPT is a term coined to describe a new method of producing and inventing that is important enough to have a protracted aggregate impact. Electricity and information technology (IT) probably are the two most important GPTs to date (Jovanovic and Rousseau, 2005).
27 The sample includes 29 SSA countries.

Business environment rating (1=low to 6=high)

Efficiency of revenue mobilization rating (1=low to 6=high)

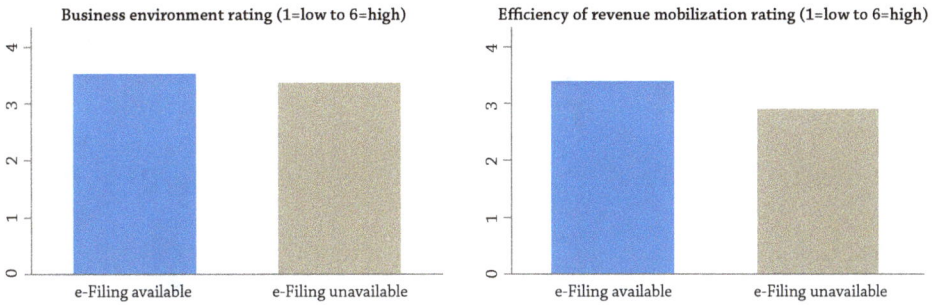

Sources: WBG GTMI 2020 data, OECD Tax Statistics 2020 data, WBG CPIA 2021 data, Doing Business 2020 data, and authors' calculations

Note: * The GTMI 2020 data are extracted from the 2022 version of the dataset which includes converted 2020 and 2022 data.

2.2.1. Taxation of the digital economy

The digital revolution offers opportunities to increase tax revenue by broadening VAT or sales taxes bases or adopting new direct digital service taxes. Taxing digital transactions is a potential and effective revenue generation strategy that could lead African countries to collect substantial revenue and create fiscal space, especially as the region's e-commerce revenue is expected to significantly increase in 2025 to US$46 100 million, compared with US$7 721 million in 2017 (a 497 percent growth rate over that period, Figure 18).[28] The use of electronic billing machines allows the automatic capture of transactions and limits the risk of fraud and tax disputes. Countries like Côte d'Ivoire, Ghana, the Republic of Congo, Uganda, and Zimbabwe tax digital financial services with an excise tax on money transfers. Although imposing mobile money levies could be controversial from the financial inclusion perspective,[29] it can generate more revenue, at least in the short-term. Sub-Saharan Africa leads the world in mobile money accounts per capita (both registered and active accounts), mobile money outlets, and volume of mobile money transactions. Close to 10 percent of GDP in transactions occur through mobile money, compared with just 7 percent of GDP in Asia and less than 2 percent of GDP in other regions (Adrian and Pazarbasioglu, 2019). Income, gains, and transactions involving cryptocurrencies are taxable in jurisdictions under capital gains tax, wealth and inheritance taxes, consumption taxes (VAT and sales taxes), transfer tax,[30] and carbon tax (to address the externalities linked to carbon emissions resulting from the important energy consumption involved in mining).[31]

---

28 Several sub-Saharan African countries, such as South Africa, Kenya, and Cameroon, have broadened their VAT and countries like Nigeria and Zimbabwe have introduced new direct digital service taxes to tax the digital economy.

29 The regressive tax measures could have significant impact on poorer households and reduce financial inclusion.

30 India has a transfer tax (one percent surcharge) on the transfers of digital currencies.

31 In 2021, significant proportions of the population in Kenya (8.5 percent), South Africa (7.1 percent) and Nigeria (6.3 percent) held digital currencies (UNCTAD, 2022). Bitcoin is legal tender in the Central African Republic.

Figure 18: Online business-to-consumer (B2C) sales of physical goods in Africa from 2017 to 2025 (US$ million)

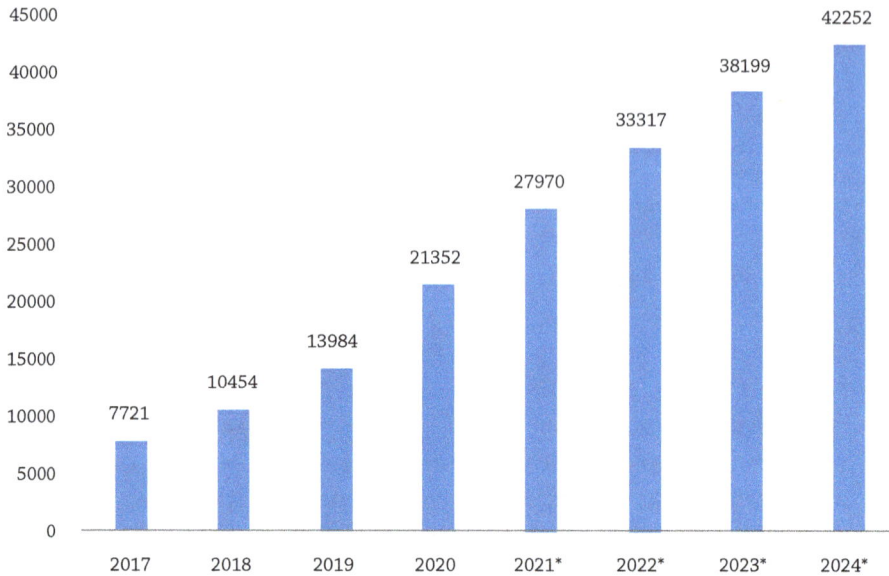

Sources: OECD/WBG/ATAF (2023) and data from Statista (2021), E-commerce revenue in Africa in 2017 to 2025 (Statista, 2021)
Note: * forecast

2.2.2. Digitalization of tax administration and modernization of tax systems

Technology could assist tax administrations in improving identification and registration of taxable entities including individuals and properties. The use of digital technologies is a means to expand the property tax base, ensuring that all properties are captured in the database. Tanzania used drone technology to support a reform strategy centered on building out a fiscal cadaster in Zanzibar. The individual property information of 13 232 buildings was collected through field data collection and on-the-ground inspections, and this was an achievement given that the property tax system under the 1934 Ordinance had only 1 370 buildings on the tax roll (World Bank, 2020). The automatic exchange of information for tax purposes between jurisdictions allows countries to revisit the designs of their capital income tax systems and tax household savings more coherently (OECD, 2021b). By facilitating cooperation and creating synergies between the tax, customs, and treasury administrations, digitalization can enhance transparency.

Domestic tax compliance costs have been estimated at 2 percent to 10 percent of the tax revenue, representing up to 2.5 percent of GDP (Evans, 2003). According to a 2007 World Bank estimate, the use of digital tools could lead to a reduction of tax collection costs by 30 percent.[32] The Rwanda Revenue Authority (RRA) has improved its administrative efficiency by cutting the cost of tax collection from 3.5 percent of total revenue in 2010 to 2.7 percent in 2018 (Better Than Cash Alliance, 2020). The modernization of the tax administration could ease the administrative burden, reduce errors due to manual inputting, and save tax collection time. It might also reduce the risk of corruption and bribery by minimizing in-person interactions between taxpayers and tax officers. The website of the revenue authority could also provide up-to-date information on tax laws and tax administration procedures for registration, filing and payment of tax, hence facilitating compliance. Reminding taxpayers through digital tools of the deadline for filing tax returns reduces the room for non-compliance. Mascagni and Nell's (2022) results show that modern ways of communicating with taxpayers, such as SMS and email, are more effective than letters in Rwanda. Digital technologies could also raise the level of compliance and increase tax collection efficiency by allowing tracking and fighting tax evasion more effectively through data analytics. The use of different electronic sources of information on taxpayer behavior should facilitate identifying high-risk taxpayer financial transactions and thereby audit priorities. Thus, digitalization could increase audit efficiency and lead to more efficient use of resources.

Technology could significantly enhance voluntary tax compliance by reducing tax filing and payment times. The effort required to file and pay taxes, including travelling (travel time and transportation costs) and queuing at the tax office, could be decreased.[33] Taxpayers also pay fewer bribes, as the reduction of visits to tax offices limits opportunities for rent-seeking activities. Also, the use of mobile money services makes it easy for taxpayers to meet their obligations, especially as more than half of the population in Africa has limited or no access to traditional banking.[34] Thus, the possibility of paying tax through mobile money transactions could be an effective way of reducing the compliance burden, notably on small taxpayers who often bear disproportionate tax compliance costs in Africa (Bruce-Twum, Schutte and Asare, 2022; Bruce-Twum and Schutte, 2021). The increased transparency that digitalization of tax systems can bring[35] could increase

---

32 More recent estimates also suggest that digitalization reduced compliance costs in South Korea by 19 percent in the 2011–2016 period.

33 The introduction of electronic billing machines (EBMs) in Rwanda has decreased the time it takes businesses to file VAT returns from 45 to 5 hours (Better Than Cash Alliance, 2020).

34 International Trade Administration (2021) data.

35 Digital technologies overcome information barriers which can improve monitoring (both by citizens through regular feedback on service quality and governments through better management of government workers) and citizen coordination (World Bank, 2016, cited in Aker, 2017).

taxpayer satisfaction and confidence in revenue authorities and governments, thereby increasing tax morale and compliance. Moreover, it is important to create digital synergies between the data networks of key entities to allow their respective data to communicate, thus expanding the tax base through third-party data and allowing pre-filled tax returns (e.g., tax administrations, customs, bank, water and electricity companies, chamber of commerce, national ID agency).

The benefits of the use of ICT go beyond improving customs and tax administrations. Digitalization may strengthen the business environment by reducing the burden of tax compliance. A 10 percent reduction in tax administration burden can lead to an increase of nearly 4 percent in entrepreneurial activity (OECD, 2021c). Also, the possibility of saving tax payment time through digital payments could encourage small business owners, especially female entrepreneurs (who often need to balance work and domestic activities), to formalize their activities. In addition, the digitalization of tax systems by enhancing data accuracy and availability could improve fiscal policy formulation in terms of revenue forecasting and budget preparation. The use of taxpayers' information could allow governments to better target income redistribution. Moreover, the implementation of digital tools enables a significant reduction of paper use, energy, and transport and contributes to environmental sustainability.

2.3. Environmental constraints to reaping digital dividends and tax challenges of the digitalizing economy

2.3.1. Environmental constraints to reaping digital dividends

While the use of digital technologies provides a promising way of raising significant tax revenue, critical environmental barriers in Africa limit its vast potential. The success of customs and tax administration modernization heavily depends on the environment. Lack of appropriate infrastructure and internet connectivity, digital literacy and training, confidence in government, adoption by tax officials and taxpayers, and lack of adequate legislation and political leadership are major constraints to the effectiveness of technology reforms in African countries.

Although access to electricity is a prerequisite for using digital tools, 600 million people, or 70 percent of the continent's population, lack access to electricity.[36] Even though access to the internet is increasingly widespread in the region, internet connection is poor and unstable in several countries, and disparity exists within countries. In addition, tax administrations experience

---

36 Sida (2023) data.

IT system outages. These factors may hinder the effective adoption of technology by taxpayers, especially those living in remote rural areas. Also, basic mobile data plans are often not affordable[37] and could hamper the deployment of technologies. Moreover, the introduction of e-levies on mobile money transactions can discourage taxpayers, particularly small taxpayers, from making digital tax payments. Anyidoho et al. (2022) show that the Ghana mobile money tax introduced in 2022 is highly regressive, meaning that it impacts the poor and lowest earners disproportionately compared to higher earners. Mobile money revenues declined by 28 percent between 2022 and 2023 in Ghana.[38]

Low digital literacy and lack of taxpayer training create a barrier to the adoption of digital tools. Obert et al. (2018) identified the knowledge gap as a major determinant of the underutilization of electronic tax filing systems in Zimbabwe. The wide digital gender gap in SSA highlights the need for more training targeted towards women. Users of e-filing and e-payment facilities are generally better educated and more sophisticated taxpayers. Thus, the modernization of the tax administration could leave a large share of the population behind and reinforce socio-economic disparities in the taxpayer population. And while criminals have already proven to be remarkably adept at attacking tax systems (Gupta et al., 2017), taxpayers may also avoid adopting technology due to mistrust of the tax administration. Digitalization raises issues about the quality of government institutions and the security and privacy of data collected for tax purposes. More digitalization may well prove counterproductive in countries with bad institutions, higher levels of corruption, more authoritarian regimes, little or no rule of law, and no protection of the privacy of their citizens. Indeed, greater use of information can also enable bad governments to better realize bad policy objectives (Jacobs, 2017).

Tax and customs officers may also resist using new technology. Tax administration staff resistance could be due to lack of adequate skills and training in using new technology and making the best use of tax data. As displayed in Figure 19, ICT expenditure (as a percentage of operating spending) in sub-Saharan Africa is not particularly different from other regions. However, in terms of human capital, most SSA countries lag behind countries in other regions.

---

37 In late 2019 (2020 Finance Act), the government of Chad removed the 18% excise duty on mobile internet (implemented in 2017) to facilitate improvements in access and usage.

38 "MTN released its annual results for 2022, and we see the impact clearly: though the levy was only imposed on the 22nd of May, mobile money revenues declined by 12% for the 6 months ending June 2022 and by 28% between H2 2021 and H2 2022" (Esselaar, 2023).

Figure 19: Levels of ICT expenditure and human capital

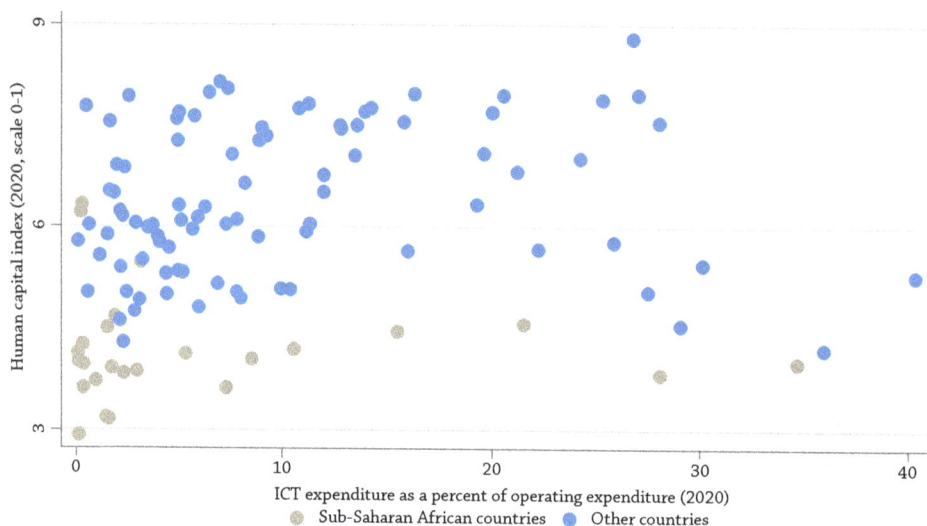

Sources: WDI and CIAT, IMF, IOTA, OECD (2022) International Survey on Revenue Administration, and authors' calculations

On the other hand, tax officers may have appropriate digital skills and sufficient infrastructure and continue to use manual and discretionary procedures. They could be resistant to change and reorganization of their work. What tends to be more likely, however, is for such resistance to be driven by the possibility of losing private benefits (through bribes) they could solicit or embezzling tax money using their discretionary powers. Although the use of technology in tax and customs administrations may reduce the risk of corruption, evidence shows that it can also facilitate corrupt practices. Chalendard *et al.* (2021) applied a novel methodology to detect corruption in Madagascar's Port of Toamasina, discovering that accomplices in the IT department of customs systematically steered the declarations of certain brokers to certain inspectors, who would in turn fail to impose penalties and fines. Their results showed that 10 percent of declarations were handled by inspectors that had not been randomly assigned, and tax revenue losses associated with this corruption scheme were approximately 3 percent of total taxes collected. Moreover, the use of electronic cash registers led to the development of automated sales suppression devices (zappers).

A lack of political leadership and supporting legal framework may further limit the ability of African tax administrations to take advantage of opportunities offered by digitalization and expose them to legal and policy risks. Without appropriate, effective, enforced, and updated legal and regulatory frameworks, namely concerning data sharing between the revenue authority, other public entities, and private actors, technology reforms cannot succeed. Qualitative evidence shows how the Malawi Revenue Authority is constrained from introducing e-filing services, given that the tax code is still silent on how to regulate such services (Santoro *et al.* (forthcoming), as cited in Okunogbe and Santoro, 2022). The existence of gaps and loopholes in taxation rules in SSA countries has made them vulnerable to base erosion and profit shifting, and digitalization has intensified these challenges with the emergence of new ways of working and types of assets.

2.3.2. *Tax challenges of the digitalizing economy*

The digitalization of the economy means that physical presence is not always needed and that more and more services can be *exported* with very limited physical presence (Leduc and Michielse, 2021). In this sense, the digital economy offers scope for profit shifting to low-tax jurisdictions, creating difficulties for countries to protect their tax bases. Tax challenges associated with digitalization affect both tax design and administration. The direct tax challenges relate to the question of how taxing rights on income generated from cross-border activities should be allocated among jurisdictions. African countries, along with other developing countries, are struggling to protect their tax bases from erosion due to practices such as the elimination or reduction of tax by multinational enterprises (MNEs) through avoiding having a taxable presence in market jurisdictions. These harmful tax practices are facilitated by provisions in domestic tax laws and double tax treaties ratified by SSA countries. Thus, MNEs can relocate their financial activities across jurisdictions to ensure they benefit from low withholding tax rates or exemption from withholding tax payment on their outward cross border payments.[39] MNEs may also eliminate or reduce their taxes by locating functions, assets, or risks in intermediate jurisdictions with preferential tax regimes. In the context of the digital economy, the rights in intangibles and their related returns can be assigned and transferred among associated enterprises, and may be transferred, sometimes for a less-than-arm's length price, to an affiliate in a country where income subsequently earned from those intangibles is subject to unduly low or no tax (OECD, 2015). Moreover, MNEs can also use such sophisticated techniques to eliminate or reduce taxes in the country of residence.

---

39 Traditionally, double tax treaties were signed to prevent no taxation or double taxation of the same income in partner jurisdictions. However, several SSA countries have signed treaties with reduced withholding tax (WHT) rates on the payments of dividends, interests, and royalties, and including other provisions curtailing their taxing rights to attract foreign direct investment. Though, research found no evidence substantiating expectations of a corresponding benefit regarding additional investment generation (Beer and Loeprick, 2018). However, treaty shopping can be particularly harmful to these countries, impairing their efforts for domestic resource mobilization and achieving sustainable development goals (Millán-Narotzky *et al.*, 2021).

VAT challenges of the digital economy relate to effective VAT collection on cross-border trade. Traditional VAT laws may lack provisions to tax supplies of services and intangibles by non-resident suppliers, especially services delivered to private consumers remotely (streaming music, broadcasting, on-demand television) and internet-based services (e.g., Microsoft Teams, Webex, and Skype calls). The destination principle is the international norm,[40] generally accepted for applying VAT to cross-border transactions. However, as digitalization enables businesses to conduct activities within a jurisdiction without having a physical activity or having a physical presence, tax compliance problems related to the identification of transactions, allocation of the taxing rights of remote supplies of services and intangibles, tax uncertainty and complexity may arise. Concerning the taxation of goods, although it is easier to determine the jurisdiction of intermediate or final consumption (physical destination of the goods) and enforce tax compliance through physical controls at customs, tax administrative and collection costs could significantly increase due to important volumes of low-value goods purchased abroad by domestic customers. Some African countries provide a VAT exemption on low-value goods (low-value consignments) given that the VAT revenue collected on these transactions is often lower than the tax collection cost. However, as e-commerce continues to expand, African governments, like governments in other regions, are becoming more concerned about the VAT revenue foregone because of these exemptions, especially as value-added tax is the largest source of tax revenue in SSA. These exemptions create distortions and increase the large VAT gap due to weaknesses in collecting VAT on domestic transactions. Of 24 African countries with adequate data, 12 had a VAT gap of 50 percent or more in 2018 (UNECA, 2019).

Tax challenges associated with digitalization also concern the prominence of digital financial assets. The recent global development of crypto assets raises issues in both tax design and implementation, notably the use of virtual currencies for both investment and speculative purposes. The challenges also arise from their decentralization, anonymity, and extra-territoriality. Tax systems were not designed for a world in which assets could be traded, and transactions completed, in anything other than national currencies (Baer *et al.*, 2023). According to the IMF African Dept. (2022), only one-quarter of countries in the SSA region have any type of regulation in place for cryptocurrencies.

---

40 The principle allows the retention of value-added taxes by the country where the taxed product is sold.

2.3.3. Multilateral efforts to address the tax challenges associated with digitalization

The taxation of the digitalized economy lies at the heart of the debate in international tax negotiations. The critical role of multilateralism in addressing the tax challenges posed by the digital revolution is well recognized. Like other countries across the globe, African countries have taken the initiative to join or create a range of international and regional bodies contributing to reforming international tax rules to protect and broaden their tax bases. Since the expansion of the Global Forum on Transparency and Exchange of Information for Tax Purposes (Global Forum) membership to non-OECD members in 2009, it has been joined by 36 African countries (31 from the SSA region) with the objective of addressing tax evasion and improving transparency and the exchange of information for tax purposes. Then, in 2014, the African members of the Global Forum decided to create the Africa Initiative aiming at addressing the specific needs and priorities of African countries to grow their information exchange capacities. In the same year, the African Tax Administration Forum (ATAF) also established the Cross-border Taxation Technical Committee (CBT) with the purpose of influencing international tax negotiations and ensuring new international tax rules reflect Africa's priorities. In 2015, the members of the Addis Tax Initiative committed to scaling up international tax cooperation through the Addis Ababa Action Agenda (AAAA) during the United Nations' third conference on Financing for Development. Since 2016, African countries have been gradually joining the OECD Base Erosion and Profit Shifting (BEPS) Inclusive Framework (23 SSA countries), whose purpose is to ensure jurisdiction collaboration on the implementation of 15 measures/actions to tackle tax avoidance, enhance transparency and improve the coherence of international tax rules. Besides the UN and the OECD, international organizations like the World Bank Group and the International Monetary Fund are engaged in supporting countries around the world to tackle tax avoidance and strengthen the capacity of developing countries to protect their tax bases.

To combat tax challenges, the international community is providing standards, technical assistance, experience, knowledge, and information sharing, as well as sharing tools with governments to address these problems effectively. Solutions to these challenges is the primary area of focus of the OECD BEPS Action Plan (Action 1). The OECD has elaborated a two-pillar solution: pillar one aims to ensure that the profits of MNEs are reallocated to their market jurisdictions; pillar two institutes a global minimum corporate tax at a rate of 15 percent. This two-pillar solution has been agreed upon by 138 countries, including 21 SSA countries. Regarding treaty abuse, a multilateral instrument

(MLI) was developed for jurisdictions to amend their tax treaties and prevent base erosion and profit shifting. The MLI has been ratified by 100 jurisdictions, including 12 SSA jurisdictions. The United Nations has also devised a solution to assist developing countries in taxing income from automated digital services by adding a new article (Article 12B) to the UN Model Convention that jurisdictions could adopt in their treaties.

Multilateral efforts to address the tax challenges arising from digitalization also concern the creation of platforms such as the Platform for Collaboration on Tax (PCT) launched in 2016 jointly by the IMF, the OECD, the UN and the WBG to strengthen their collaboration on tax issues and provide guidance to developing countries through policy dialogue, technical assistance (namely in the formulation and implementation of tax reforms) and capacity building, knowledge creation, and dissemination. The PCT partners developed some technical toolkits (individually or collectively), including the IMF's Revenue Administration Gap Analysis Program (RA-GAP) and the UNDP/OECD's Tax Inspectors Without Borders (TIWB).[41] They also developed (with other development partners) the Tax Administration Diagnostic Assessment Tool (TADAT) and the International Survey on Revenue Administration (ISORA). A VAT Digital Toolkit for Africa was developed jointly by the OECD, the WBG and the ATAF in 2023 to assist African jurisdictions in designing and implementing VAT policies to tax digital trade. Regarding virtual currencies, the Financial Action Task Force standards on anti-money laundering (AML) and combating the financing of terrorism (CFT) mitigate the risks associated with virtual assets. OECD (2020) provides guidance to governments on determining the appropriate tax treatment of cryptocurrencies.[42]

2.4. Illustrative country case studies on the adoption of digital tools in customs and tax administrations

The country case studies present the experiences of the Democratic Republic of Congo, Guinea, and Rwanda in adopting digital technologies in customs and tax administration.

---

41 Support provided by TIWB in collaboration with partners like ATAF (mainly on transfer-pricing issues, criminal tax investigations, exchange, and effective use of information) increased tax revenue collected by African jurisdictions by US$1.2 billion from 2012 to 2021.

42 Other international initiatives to assist countries in protecting their tax bases include: the PCT partners' Medium Term Revenue Strategy (MTRS), the OECD Forum on Tax Administration (FTA); the Intergovernmental Forum on Mining, Metals and Sustainable Development (IGF) and partners' (like the OECD and the ATAF) technical assistance and capacity building on taxation of extractive industries; the IMF Fiscal Analysis of Resource Industries (FARI) and Tax Policy Assessment Framework (TPAF); the OECD and the World Bank Tax administration maturity models; and peer-to-peer assistance related to digitalization.

Box 1. Domestic resource mobilization in Guinea and customs digitalization

Guinea performs weakly in domestic resource mobilization with a tax-to-GDP ratio of 13.9 percent, far below the objective of government tax revenue to GDP of 20 percent that the ECOWAS member states aim to reach. Despite being endowed with abundant natural resources and experiencing a recent increase in mining exports, Guinea's resource tax revenue is not substantial. For example, the volume of bauxite exports of the economy has almost tripled over the period 2016 to 2021 and ranged from about 29.4 million to over 85.6 million tons. By contrast, the tax revenue generated from the sector declined by 30 percent from 2015 to 2020. The large size of the informal sector (estimated between 70 to 90 percent by the APIP (Agence de Promotion des Investissements Privés) contributes to the country's low tax performance. The numerous tax incentives, gaps, and loopholes in the tax legislation also contribute to the poor tax revenue performance. The quality of the tax administration's public service delivery is low, and the World Bank Country Policy and Institutional Assessment (CPIA) efficiency of revenue mobilization rating was 3.5 out of 6 in 2021 (this score has not been improved since 2016).

According to the 2021 Afrobarometer survey results, 51 percent of Guineans think that most Guinea tax officials are involved in corruption, and 45 percent of Guineans think that the government does not use the tax revenues collected to improve the wellbeing of citizens. Thus, pursuing a digital journey is seen as a means to enhance Guinean revenue authorities' performance, improve public service delivery, transparency and accountability, and limit corruption.

As electronic tax filing and electronic payment are not available in Guinea, the country experience presented here focuses on customs modernization. In June 2017, the government of Guinea decided to digitalize its customs proced-ures by issuing an Electronic Single Window system to facilitate the free flow of operations of external trade operations and boost DRM and economic growth. The initiative also intends to reduce the compliance burden on firms, facilit-ate their access to information to fulfil their obligations and minimize border compliance time and the cost associated with compliance with the country's customs regulations. The project was implemented in late 2019 by the govern-ment of Guinea in partnership with the Webb Fontaine group.

An analysis of customs revenues' trends shows that taxes on international trade increased by 151.6 percent 8 months after the technology adoption. The trade tax revenues continued to rise over the next 8 months at a rate of 31.5 percent. These results were achieved through improved customs administration performance, time and cost savings, the limitation of in-person interactions and the facilitation of fraud detection related to the use of digital tools.

The increase in revenue has reduced in recent years; however, the activation of the remaining features of the platform such as the possibility of paying tax through mobile money transactions, could increase the government revenue more significantly.

Figure 20: Taxes on international trade in US$ million

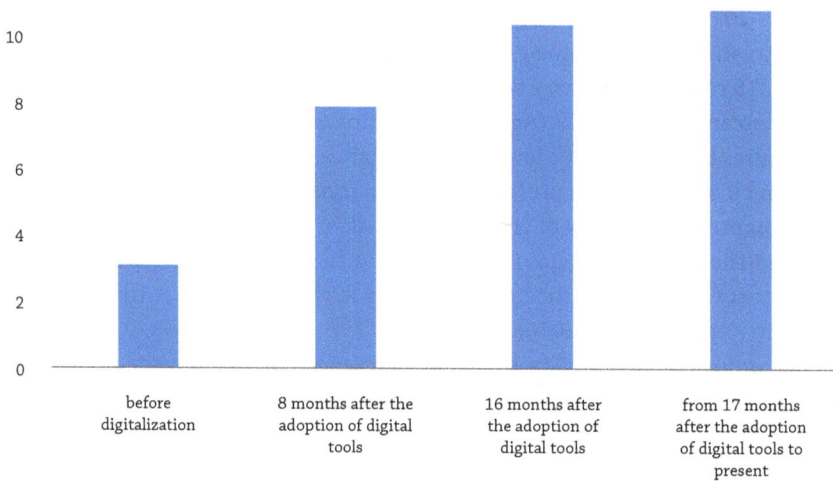

Source: Guinea Revenue Authority data and authors' calculations

Box 2. Rwanda Revenue Authority's digitalization journey

Rwanda's technological growth has evolved since the government focused on the importance of ICT as a catalyst for driving economic growth. Since the Rwanda Vision 2020 plan, the digital transformation agenda has aimed to catalyze progress across sectors, including healthcare, education, agriculture, infrastructure, and public finance management. The Rwanda Revenue Authority (RRA) aims to become an organization that is "fit for purpose": a revenue administration with efficient service delivery, data-driven decision-making, IT-powered in its operations.

Harnessing technology to drive revenue mobilization in Rwanda

The initiation of Rwanda's tax system digitalization dates back to 2004 when software was introduced to streamline taxpayer data management. This pivotal moment included the implementation of an Automated System for Customs Data (ASYCUDA) that streamlined customs procedures by enabling different agencies in the customs clearance process to work as one-stop centers (as a result, the cargo clearance times reduced from 3 days on average to a matter of hours) and set the stage for further digital advancements. The subsequent years saw the progressive introduction of a diverse array of digital services.

A significant milestone in Rwanda's digital journey unfolded in 2010 with the rollout of a nationwide fiber-optic network with an impressive coverage of over 95 percent of the entire country. Its primary objective was to establish high-speed internet accessibility throughout the country, especially in urban hubs and underserved regions. By doing so, it effectively lowered the barrier to entry for millions of Rwandans, facilitating their connectivity to the digital realm. This foundational network has served as the bedrock for strengthening internet connectivity and streamlining data transmission across Rwanda. The government took proactive measures to bridge the digital divide by equipping students and communities with essential digital competencies and ensuring access to computers through various initiatives. Moreover, to harness the full spectrum of advantages brought by digitization, Rwanda has strategically used its tax policy to promote the adoption and utilization of technological devices. This strategic approach encompasses various policy measures, including the exemption of ICT equipment such as telephones. Additionally, Rwanda has implemented a gradual increment in taxes, particularly excise taxes on telecommunications (airtime). This incremental approach will see the tax rate climb from 3 percent to 5 percent, further to 8 percent, eventually reaching 10 percent over a span of ten years.

In 2011 the online registration, e-filing, and e-payment systems were launched, ushering in an era where taxpayers could fulfil their responsibilities remotely, effectively eliminating the need for in-person interactions with RRA officers. This transition yielded profound outcomes, with the number of registered taxpayers growing five times between 2011 and 2019, fostering a more inclusive tax environment. The transition to digital interface not only facilitated seamless tax compliance but also established an efficient reconciliation between tax collection and online payments, thus leading to a reduction in collection costs. In 2012, the implementation of an online declaration system for imports streamlined the importation process, substantially curtailing time and costs associated with customs clearance, thereby fostering a more efficient trade environment. Presently, e-filing is used at 100 percent of all tax types, while e-payments are utilized for 98 percent of all tax transactions.

Subsequently in 2013, Rwanda introduced the use of EBMs, or electronic billing machines, for VAT-registered taxpayers. This transformative system enables businesses to issue electronic receipts for goods and services, transmitting transaction data to the RRA in real time. The positive impacts of this initiative on the tax collection system are palpable, with VAT revenues experiencing an approximate 30 percent improvement in its inaugural year of implementation. Also, the improved accuracy and transparency of transaction data led to a more than 80 percent reduction in the time businesses spent on filling VAT returns. The introduction of EBMs in Rwanda has reduced fraudulent value-added tax (VAT) claims by 25-35 percent (Better Than Cash Alliance, 2020). The use of EBMs has since extended to non-VAT taxpayers to improve transparency in monitoring and collecting other tax types, such as corporate income tax (CIT), where, for instance, expenses are validated only when supported by an EBM invoice, with minimal exceptions.

The benefit in EBM introduction is not only enjoyed by the tax administration but the taxpayer as well, who have access to their stock movement and sales, making personal monitoring and submission of tax returns easy. In 2019, the RRA launched live chat support for taxpayers. Furthermore, Rwanda has taken progressive steps to encourage the adoption of mobile money transfers and foster a cashless economy. One significant measure is the exemption of taxes on mobile money transfers, which not only incentivizes individuals to embrace digital financial transactions but also supports the broader goal of reducing reliance on physical cash, thus enhancing economic efficiency. Importantly, these policies have played a pivotal role in reinforcing the effectiveness of tax administration and revenue collection in Rwanda. Temporary suspensions of upstream revenue collection have been strategically leveraged to yield substantial benefits in terms of revenue generation and collection efficiency.

The tax digitalization journey has also led to the adoption by the RRA of a new operating model that is not just IT-driven but more so data-driven (for instance to discard the door-to-door approaches of recruiting and enforcing non-compliance to risk-based interventions and high reliance on data analytics). The RRA uses analytics and has implemented an "automated audit case" selection process since 2017 to improve audit efficiency. The pinnacle of digitization involves real-time integration and analysis of data from various sources, such as banks, enabling the RRA to pinpoint risks, enhance audit efficiency, and extract insights beneficial for business growth and financing access. This transformation also recalibrated the role of tax professionals. Routine tasks like data gathering and verification were automated, freeing tax professionals to focus on data analysis and strategy formulation for revenue generation. This reimagined role calls for a new generation of tax professionals with backgrounds in mathematics, science, and IT engineering. This shift underscores the immense possibilities that technology ushers in for tax collection and Rwanda is poised to launch its tax administration even further by leveraging technologies like block chain, predictive and behavioral analysis to curb non-compliance before it happens, use of artificial intelligence, for example, to respond to stakeholder inquiries 24 hours a day; providing all taxpayers with a holistic view of their tax account transactions further reinstating transparency, pre-filling of all tax returns further reducing cost of compliance to the taxpayer.

The cumulative result of these efforts is evident in the substantial growth of the tax-to-GDP ratio, which increased from 11.2 percent in 2009/10 to 16 percent in 2019/20, just before the onset of the Covid-19 pandemic.

Despite its disruptive impact, the pandemic had a limited impact on revenue collection during the period 2020-2021 due to the advanced digitalization of the RRA's system that enabled taxpayers to seamlessly fulfil their tax obligations without physically visiting RRA offices. In the FY2022/23, the use of technology in tax administration by the RRA has significantly improved tax compliance with reported turnovers increasing from Rwf37.8 billion in FY2021/2022 to Rwf110.5 billion in FY2022/23. Corporate income tax increased from Rwf0.25 billion in the previous fiscal year to Rwf0.73 billion in FY22/23 all these as a result of bringing on board new taxpayers to digital platforms.

Moreover, the outcome has been a considerable enhancement in governance transparency and responsiveness, achieved by streamlining public services and reducing bureaucratic inefficiencies. Most notably, this approach has spurred socio-economic transformation.

Beyond revenue collection

Beyond their conventional role in revenue collection and tax compliance, the use of technologies for taxation has evolved into a vital source of data that can be converted into information and knowledge that enable decision-making and data-driven policy formulation by the tax authority and the government at large.

A striking illustration are the insights collected from data harvested through EBMs. This information serves as more than just mere transactional records, but as information for analysing supply chains, thereby shaping Rwanda's trade and industrial policies. Data from EBMs are also being used for different policy formulation purposes by government agencies. Another specific example is the use of EBM data to conduct economic analysis that will ensure coordination of the fiscal and monetary policies spearheaded by the Ministry of Finance and

Economic Planning and the Central Bank of Rwanda. Even during the tumult of Covid-19, daily data collection by EBMs played a pivotal role in tracking economic activity, thus empowering the government to formulate judicious decisions while concurrently implementing vital social distancing measures.

The fusion of technology and governance has also improved the business climate in Rwanda, fostering a symbiotic relationship between the government and the private sector, and opening avenues for swift policy adjustments while mitigating opportunities for corruption and reducing the cost of compliance, among other benefits.

Figure 21: Tax-to-GDP ratio, percent of GDP

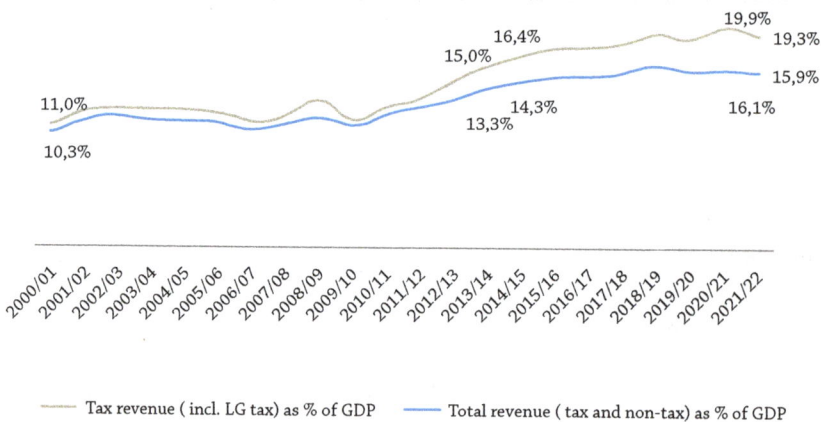

Source: Rwanda Revenue Authority data and authors' calculations

Box 3. The DRC's customs and tax system, and digitalization journey

The tax system of the Democratic Republic of Congo is inefficient and complex. The country's tax-to-GDP ratio reached only 8.1 percent in 2021. The low tax performance of the DRC is related to factors such as the large size of the informal sector, the multiplicity of taxes, and the granting of numerous tax exemptions, which make the tax system complex and increase the burden for both tax officers and taxpayers. The country has more than 240 different taxes and levies at the central level, and the average annual time to comply with tax law measures in the DRC reached 346 hours in 2021. The DRC relies heavily on mining and forestry revenue. Despite recent improvements in transparency in the mining sector through the disclosure of mining contracts, significant governance challenges remain (World Bank, 2023).

The modernization of revenue authorities is a key priority of the DRC's Public Finance Reform Strategic Plan 2022–2028. The implementation of electronic filing is in progress, and the country also intends to adopt a biometric taxpayer identification system. The country's digitalization journey is pioneered by customs modernization supported by development partners. To date, the DRC continues the implementation of the ASYCUDA across customs points of entry and the digitalization of government payments through ISYS-REGIES. The Government Financial Data Exchange Network (REDOFIE) platform, adopted by the DRC Government, has created synergies between the different revenue authorities including the tax authority (Direction Générale des Impôts (DGI)), the customs authority (Direction Générale des Douanes et Accises (DGDA)), and the Direction Générale des Recettes Administratives, Judiciaires, Domaniales et de Participations (DGRAD) in charge of collecting non-tax revenue and other government agencies. The government continues to extend the platform across the country.

The DRC also has a physical digital space which serves as a repository of financial information used to conduct data analytics. Further, the Democratic Republic of Congo plans to deploy systematic cross-checks of data in order to facilitate fraud detection and compliance risk management.

2.5. Key lessons for successful ICT reforms in tax administration

This section provides policymakers with key lessons for successful ICT reforms in tax administration learned from the experiences of African countries and international peers. Each nation's digitalization journey is unique and should be based on the needs and maturity of the revenue authority and adapted to the local environment. While some countries, like Rwanda, Mauritius, adopted new technologies quickly, others such as the United States, and the United Kingdom have opted for a long-term, gradual digital transformation journey. The success of technology reforms lies in defining a clear and wider vision and a digitalization strategy covering the regulatory, human resources, and financial aspects. Also, being user-centric in focusing on the needs of taxpayers during the design phase of digitalization is key to the success of ICT reforms in tax administration.

As stated in the previous section, access to electricity and reliable internet are prerequisites to e-filing and e-payment. Thus, improving electricity supply and internet connectivity are essential to the adoption of digital technologies. Obert *et al.* (2018) found that power cuts and non-availability of the internet caused the underutilization of electronic tax filing systems in Zimbabwe. The government of Rwanda and donors massively invested in a nationwide fiber optic backbone which facilitates the transfer of high-speed data across the country, and the Rwanda Revenue Authority became one of the first to test the technology (Schreiber, 2018). The success of technology reforms strongly depends on the existence of enabling and supportive regulatory and business environments. ICT reforms must be supported by the introduction of new and appropriate legal and regulatory frameworks inspiring users' trust and confidence in the integrity and security of the systems, notably concerning the privacy and safety of data. The new regulation must also cover data sharing between revenue authorities.

A proper procurement process and investment in the right technology tool by selecting between in-house software development and off-the-shelf solutions (or a combination of both) are determinant in ensuring the success of technology reforms. It is also important to build an internal ICT capacity that could ensure the maintenance, development, and enhancement of IT systems. Focusing on the needs of taxpayers during the design phase of digitalization, namely by proposing appropriate payment solutions and digital tools, is key to success in modernizing the tax administration. Kenya has pioneered the use of mobile-based electronic payment services to facilitate e-payment to taxpayers, especially those who do not have traditional bank accounts. Introducing mandatory electronic billing machines could be challenging as evidenced by challenges Rwanda faced during its rollout. After the initial experience, the country transitioned to a computer-based solution, which also encountered challenges in implementation, as not all taxpayers are able to use computers. This highlights the importance of experimentation. Digital systems should be tested before being implemented.

Institutional and operational reforms are needed. High-level leadership support is necessary for the success of the modernization of the tax administration. Senior leaders of tax administrations must support the digitalization journey by being flexible and open to change and great motivators. Staff may need training before implementing the technology. Investment in human resources is crucial to ensure the effective and proper use of digital tools by tax officers. An assessment of the tax administration staff's capacity and skills will help identify training needs. Taxpayers may also be reluctant to use new technologies due to a lack of digital literacy. It is crucial that governments invest in education and training sessions to ensure that citizens take up digital technology. Tax administrations must also provide taxpayers with training and sensitization programs which could help the latter use e-filing and e-payment. Transition time and related costs should also be factored into digitalization plans.

As female digital literacy is particularly low in Africa, targeted and adapted training towards women is recommended. Taxpayer engagement is key to success in adopting technologies and could be enhanced by facilitating access to information on tax laws and procedures through modern and traditional communication methods. By making taxpayers' online and offline interactions personalized, simple, consistent, intuitive, and delivered in real time, tax administrations can build a 360° view of taxpayers and their needs, helping them customize e-services and open omnichannel communications (Microsoft and PwC, 2018). Taxpayer engagement is also key to tax morale and voluntary compliance and could limit recourse to technology-enabled mass registrations[43] taking place in sub-Saharan African countries. Alm et al.'s (2010) study on tax compliance behavior showed that customer-friendly tax administration increased average compliance by 27 percent.

Peer-to-peer collaboration with other tax administrations to learn from their experiences, collaboration with regional and international partners and the use of the technical toolkits they developed could also support African countries in their digitalization journey. The World Bank Tax Diamond and the FTA (Forum on Tax Administration) Digital Transformation Maturity Model could help tax administrations understand and assess their human and institutional capacity gaps. Diamond allows countries to self-evaluate and determine their infrastructure investment needs, assess the ICT landscape of their tax administration and customs, and improve their methodologies for business process reengineering and business process mapping (Junquera-Varela et al., 2022). The Research Department in the African Tax Administration Forum (ATAF) Secretariat has also produced a guidebook to improve ICT acquisition, implementation, and maintenance by African countries. Moreover, the Inventory of Tax Technology Initiatives (ITTI) launched by the OECD, IMF, and other partners like the CREDAF[44] and ATAF, provides information on digitalization practices and initiatives implemented by tax administrations.

2.6. Toward higher levels of digitalization or digital maturity

To harness the potential of technology, it is recommended that tax authorities fully exploit the large amount of data they can access and improve their practices to reach higher levels of digitalization or digital maturity following

---

43 Aggressive expansion of tax registration numbers is highly likely to result in the registration mainly of small-scale enterprises that will, in practice, pay little or no tax (Moore, 2020).
44 CREDAF (Cercle de Réflexion et d'Echange des Dirigeants des Administrations Fiscales), or Exchange and Research Centre for Leaders of Tax Administrations, was formally launched in 1982 aiming at facilitating good practice exchanges among tax administration leaders of 30 French speaking countries including 20 SSA countries.

a well-defined transformational strategy. Digital maturity refers to the level of digitalization of tax authority procedures (Junquera-Varela *et al.*, 2022). Investing in human resources, data quality, analytics, and compliance risk management models could significantly increase tax revenue and improve tax administration management and the efficiency of tax collection.

Technology substantially supports tax authorities in identifying and registering taxable entities (individuals and properties). The use of ICT tools provides tax administrations with a complete and comprehensive taxpayer registry and strengthens their capacity to tax personal income and assets. However, in SSA countries, taxpayers may have various identification numbers for different purposes, increasing the administrative burden. By contrast, the use of a unique digital taxpayer identifier allows the taxpayer to authenticate themselves to access information and services securely. The single digital identity solution could reduce operational costs and ensure that all parts of the organization have the same level of information regarding taxpayers, thereby facilitating fraud detection. Digital identity could be created securely using biometrics. In Estonia, the government issued the first digital identity cards about 20 years ago. To date, all Estonian and e-residents have digital identity cards developed using blockchain technology.[45] Among the African Union's specific objectives to drive digital transformation and propel industrialization is the issuance of a digital legal identity for 99.9 percent of African people by 2030.

Furthermore, the creation of synergies between the different revenue authorities (tax, customs, and treasury administrations) through technology facilitates tax enforcement and leads to better accountability for results. The use of the single digital identity allows matching the relevant tax and customs data to obtain comprehensive information on taxpayers' liabilities. The Democratic Republic of Congo's REDOFIE platform, implemented 3 years ago, has created synergies between the different revenue authorities and other government agencies. Non-compliance could be identified through automatic crosschecks of this information with the content of tax returns and customs declarations. More ambitious governments with higher maturity levels could even move to a central single-platform approach by linking individuals' data held by different public agencies. DRC has a physical digital space which serves as a repository of financial information. MyInfo, available in Singapore, is an example of a single digital space that serves as a one-stop repository of an individual's information, such as income, housing, and contact details from both government-verified and user-provided data (OECD, 2019). Moreover,

---

45 Estonia is one the most advanced countries in terms of digital identity management. The country also has an e-Residency program allowing anyone who (regardless of citizenship or location) wishes to become an e-resident of Estonia and access the jurisdiction's diverse digital services.

tax authorities could collaborate with the private sector, especially digital platforms, to access the vast amount of data on consumption and income they hold, which could serve fraud detection. Digital identities could also be used across borders to detect transnational fraud. At the customs level, mirror analysis allows the reconciling of a jurisdiction's import declaration data with exports reported by its economic partner jurisdictions, and the discrepancies detected may serve for post-clearance audit purposes.

Using predictive and prescriptive analytics in tax administrations, and building risk management models lead to a more transparent and efficient selection of cases for audit. The Kenyan iTax system has enabled the Kenya Revenue Authority to easily generate weekly, monthly, quarterly, or yearly revenue and audit reports (Ndung'u, 2017). Practical use of analytics also helps identify tax avoidance and fraud schemes. As mentioned earlier, by applying a novel methodology to Madagascar customs data, Chalendard *et al.* (2021) detected a corruption scheme used by tax officers. Disaggregated tax collection data may also serve to evaluate the tax administration's own performance, conduct tax gap analyses and modeling the impact of tax policies, namely by collaborating with researchers. The recent upsurge in the literature on taxation in low- and middle-income countries is largely due to the availability of administrative tax data in electronic format (Okunogbe and Santoro, 2022). At a broader level, real-time access to this data can better inform policymaking at national and international levels.

2.7. Conclusion

It is well recognized that the digital revolution raises significant challenges for both tax design and administration, which are likely to increase. This chapter makes it clear that addressing these challenges requires both country-level and multilateral efforts. The chapter also presents the numerous opportunities digitalization provides to broaden the tax base and make tax revenue collection more efficient. Hence, the digital transformation of economies can improve domestic resource mobilization to support sustainable development goals.

The success of ICT reforms heavily relies on an enabling environment, and the chapter provides relevant recommendations for both African countries who want to pursue a digital journey and those who are interested in reaching higher levels of digital maturity and fully exploiting the potential of digitalization. Illustrative case studies focused on Rwanda, Guinea, and the Democratic Republic of Congo present their experiences in modernizing customs and tax administrations. Countries that want to embark on a digitalization journey must recognize the importance of high-level leadership support. Legal and regulatory frameworks need to be updated. These countries need to create favorable environments for the deployment of new technologies through inclusive investment in electricity, internet connectivity, ICT infrastructure, and human capital, as well as favorable legislative and regulatory environments. While each country's digitalization journey is unique, defining a clear and wider vision, a long-term digital transformational strategy, and opting for more supportive technologies for both the tax authority and taxpayers are key to success in modernizing the tax administration.

For countries pursuing their digital journeys, investing in human resources, data quality, analytics, and compliance risk management models could harness the potential of new technologies, improve tax collection and tax administration management. Strengthening the collaboration and information sharing between tax authorities and customs, treasury administrations, remaining public agencies, the private sector, and foreign revenue authorities is crucial to unlock the potential of new technologies. In our flourishing digital economies, data security and privacy remain significant concerns, and it is important for African countries to find an equitable trade-off between data privacy and security requirements and their use for improving tax policy effectiveness and efficiency.

References

Adrian, T. and Pazarbasioglu, C. (2019) 'Five facts on fintech,' *IMF Blog*, 27 June. Available at: https://www.imf.org/en/Blogs/Articles/2019/06/27/blog-five-facts-on-fintech

African Union (AU) (2019) *The digital transformation strategy for Africa (2020–2030)*. Addis Ababa: AU. Available at: https://au.int/sites/default/files/documents/38507-doc-DTS_for_Africa_2020-2030_English.pdf

Aker, J. C. (2017) 'Using digital technology for public service provision in developing countries', in Gupta, S. *et al.* (eds.) *Digital revolutions in public finance*. Washington, DC: IMF, pp. 201-224. Available at: https://doi.org/10.5089/9781484315224.071

Alm, J. *et al.* (2010) 'Taxpayer information assistance services and tax compliance behavior', *Journal of Economic Psychology*, 31(4), pp. 577-586.

Anyidoho, N. A. *et al.* (2022) *Mobile money taxation and informal workers: Evidence from Ghana's E-Levy*. ICTD Working paper No. 146. Brighton, UK: Institute of Development Studies. Available at: https://doi.org/10.1111/dpr.12704

Baer, K. *et al.* (2023) 'Taxing cryptocurrencies', *Oxford Review of Economic Policy*, 39(3), pp. 478-497. Available at: https://doi.org/10.1093/oxrep/grad035

Bate, A. P. (2021) 'Does digitalisation improve the mobilisation of tax revenues in Africa?', *African Multidisciplinary Tax Journal*, 2021(1), pp. 94-112. Available at: https://doi.org/10.47348/AMTJ/2021/i1a6

Beer, S. and Loeprick, J. (2018) *The cost and benefits of tax treaties with investment hubs: Findings from sub-Saharan Africa*. Policy research working paper No. 8623. Washington, DC: World Bank. Available at: https://doi.org/10.1596/1813-9450-8623

Begazo, T., Blimpo, M. and Dutz, M. A. (2023) *Digital Africa: Technological transformation for jobs*. Washington, DC: World Bank. Available at: https://www.worldbank.org/en/region/afr/publication/digital-africa

Bellon, M. *et al.* (2022) 'Digitalization to improve tax compliance: Evidence from VAT e-invoicing in Peru', *Journal of Public Economics*, 210, p. 104661. Available at: https://doi.org/10.1016/j.jpubeco.2022.104661

Better Than Cash Alliance (2020) *Tax digitalization in Rwanda: Success factors and pathways forward*. New York: Better Than Cash Alliance. Available at: https://btca-production-site.s3.amazonaws.com/document_files/527/document_files/Tax_Digitalization_in_Rwanda_Success_Factors_and_Pathways_Forward.pdf?1606765795

Bruce-Twum, E. and Schutte, D. (2021) 'Tax compliance cost of SMEs in Ghana', *Journal of Accounting, Finance and Auditing Studies*, 7(4), pp. 1-22.

Bruce-Twum, E., Schutte, D. and Asare, N. (2022) 'Determinants of tax compliance costs of small and medium enterprises in emerging economies: Evidence from Ghana', *Social Sciences & Humanities Open*, 6(2022), p. 100343.

Brun, J-F. *et al.* (2020) Are ICT's boosting tax revenues? Evidence from developing countries. Études et Documents, (9), CERDI.

Chalendard, C. *et al.* (2021) *Corruption in customs*. World Bank Group policy research working paper No. 9802. Washington, DC: World Bank Group.

CIAT, IMF, IOTA, OECD (2022) *International survey on revenue administration: 2020 and 2021*. Available at: https://data.rafit.org/?sk=8b008788-ebde-4d61-bc90-7438d6aa12dc&sId=1637191076670

Colin, N. *et al.* (2015) Économie numérique. In *Notes du conseil d'analyse économique*, 2015/7(26), pp. 1-12. Paris : Éditions Conseil d'analyse économique.

Devereux, M. P. and Vella, J. (2018) Debate: 'Implications of digitalization for international corporate tax reform', *Intertax*, 46(6/7), pp. 550-559. Available at: https://doi.org/10.54648/taxi2018056

Esselaar, S. (2023) 'Impact of Ghana's mobile money levy', *RIS Articles*, 16 March. Available at: https://researchictsolutions.com/home/impact-of-ghanas-mobile-money-levy/

European Commission (2014) *Commission expert group on taxation of the digital economy*. Brussels: European Commission. Available at: https://taxation-customs.ec.europa.eu/document/download/cb640cdf-02f6-42f3-81a2-6db6b256577c_en?filename=report_digital_economy.pdf

Evans, C. (2003) 'Studying the studies: An overview of recent research into taxation operating cost', *eJournal of Tax Research*, 1(1), pp. 64-92. Available at: http://classic.austlii.edu.au/au/journals/eJlTaxR/2003/4.html

Gupta, S. *et al.* (2017) 'Introduction: Reshaping public finance', in Gupta, S. *et al.* (eds.) *Digital revolutions in public finance*. Washington, DC: IMF, pp. 1-21. Available at: https://doi.org/10.5089/9781484315224.071

International Monetary Fund (IMF) African Dept. (2022) *Regional economic outlook. Sub-Saharan Africa: Living on the edge*. Washington, DC: International Monetary Fund.

International Trade Administration (2021) *The rise of ecommerce in Africa*. Washington, DC: International Trade Administration. Available at: https://www.trade.gov/rise-ecommerce-africa

Jacobs, B. (2017) 'Digitalization and taxation', in Gupta, S. (eds.) *Digital revolutions in public finance*. Washington, DC: International Monetary Fund, pp. 25-55. Available at: https://doi.org/10.5089/9781484315224.071

Jovanovic, B. and Rousseau, P. L. (2005) 'General purpose technologies', in Aghion, P. and Durlauf, S. (eds.), *Handbook of economic growth*. Vol. 1. Amsterdam: Elsevier, pp. 1181-1224.

Junquera-Varela, R. F. *et al.* (2022) *Digital transformation of tax and customs administrations*. EFI Insight - Governance Series. Washington, DC: World Bank.

Kochanova, A., Hasnain, Z. and Larson, B. (2020) 'Does e-government improve government capacity? Evidence from tax compliance costs, tax revenue, and public procurement competitiveness', *The World Bank Economic Review*, 34(1), pp. 101-120.

Koyuncu, C., Yilmaz, R. and Ünver, M. (2016) 'Does ICT penetration enhance tax revenue?: Panel evidence', *Anadolu Üniversitesi Sosyal Bilimler Dergisi*, 16(Özel Sayı), pp. 71-80.

Le, T. M., Pham, D. M. and De Wulf, L. (2007) *Estimating economic benefits for revenue administration reform projects*. PREM notes; no. 112. Public Sector Governance. Washington, DC: World Bank.

Leduc, S. and Michielse, G. (2021) 'Are tax treaties worth it for developing economies?', in De Mooij, R., Klemm, A. and Perry, V. (eds.) *Corporate income taxes under pressure: Why reform is needed and how it could be designed*. Washington, DC: International Monetary Fund, pp. 123-173.

Mascagni, G. and Nell, C. (2022) 'Tax compliance in Rwanda: Evidence from a message field experiment', *Economic Development and Cultural Change*, 70(2), pp. 587-623.

Microsoft and PwC (2018) *Digital transformation of tax administration*. Available at: http://info.microsoft.com/rs/157-GQE-382/images/Digital%20Transformation%20of%20Tax%20Administration%20White%20Paper.pdf

Millán-Narotzky, L. *et al.* (2021) *Tax treaty aggressiveness: Who is undermining taxing rights in Africa?* ICTD Working paper No. 125. Sussex, UK: Institute of Development Studies.

Moore, M. (2020) *What is wrong with African tax administration?* ICTD Working paper No. 111. Sussex, UK: Institute of Development Studies.

Ndung'u, N. (2017) 'Digitalization in Kenya revolutionizing tax design and revenue administration', in Gupta, S. *et al.* (eds.) *Digital revolutions in public finance*. Washington, DC: International Monetary Fund, pp. 241-257. Available at: https://doi.org/10.5089/9781484315224.071

Obert, S. *et al.* (2018) 'Effect of e-tax filing on tax compliance: A case of clients in Harare, Zimbabwe', *African Journal of Business Management*, 12(11), pp. 338-342.

Okunogbe, O. and Santoro, F. (2022) 'The promise and limitations of information technology for tax mobilization', *The World Bank Research Observer*, 38(2), pp. 295-324.

Organisation for Economic Co-operation and Development (OECD) (2015) *Addressing the tax challenges of the digital economy, Action 1 - 2015 final report*. OECD/G20 base erosion and profit shifting project. Paris: OECD Publishing. Available at: http://dx.doi.org/10.1787/9789264241046-en

OECD (2019) *Tax administration 2019: Comparative information on OECD and other advanced and emerging economies*. Paris: OECD Publishing. Available at: https://doi.org/10.1787/74d162b6-en

OECD (2020) *Taxing virtual currencies: An overview of tax treatments and emerging tax policy issues*. Paris: OECD Publishing. Available at: https://www.oecd.org/en/publications/taxing-virtual-currencies_e29bb804-en.html

OECD (2021a) *Development co-operation report 2021: Shaping a just digital transformation*. Paris: OECD Publishing. Available at: https://doi.org/10.1787/ce08832f-en

OECD (2021b) *OECD secretary-general tax report to G20 finance ministers and central bank governors*. Paris: OECD Publishing. Available at: www.oecd.org/tax/tax-policy/tax-and-fiscal-policies-after-the-covid-19-crisis.htm

OECD (2021c) *Supporting the digitalisation of developing country tax administrations*. Paris: OECD Publishing. Available at: www.oecd.org/tax/forum-on-tax-administration/publications-and-products/supporting-the-digitalisation-of-developing-country-taxadministrations.htm

OECD (2022) *Revenue statistics in Africa 2022*. Paris: OECD Publishing. Available at: https://www.compareyourcountry.org/tax-revenues-africa

OECD/WBG/ATAF (2023) *VAT digital toolkit for Africa*. Paris: OECD Publishing. Available at: https://web-archive.oecd.org/2023-06-27/651045-vat-digital-toolkit-for-africa.pdf

Santoro, F. *et al.* (Forthcoming) From hand to mouse redux: Data, technology and tax administration in Africa: A review of existing evidence. ICTD Working Paper Series.

Schreiber, L. (2018) *The foundation for reconstruction: Building the Rwanda Revenue Authority, 2001-2017*. Princeton University Innovations for Successful Societies, Princeton University. Available at: https://successfulsocieties.princeton.edu/sites/g/files/toruqf5601/files/LS_Rwanda_Tax_Formatted_5.29.18jgToU962018_1.pdf

Swedish International Development Cooperation Agency (Sida) (2023) Power Africa. *Swedish International Development Cooperation Agency*. Available at: https://www.sida.se/en/for-partners/private-sector/power-africa

United Nations (UN) (2021) *COVID-19 and e-commerce a global review*. New York: United Nations.

United Nations Conference on Trade and Development (UNCTAD) (2022) *All that glitters is not gold: The high cost of leaving cryptocurrencies unregulated*. UNCTAD policy brief No. 100. Geneva: UNCTAD.

United Nations Economic Commission for Africa (UNECA) (2019) *Economic report on Africa 2019: Fiscal policy for financing sustainable development in Africa*. Addis Ababa: UNECA.

World Bank (2016) *World development report 2016: Digital dividends*. Washington, DC: World Bank Group.

World Bank (2020a) *Doing business database*. Available at: https://databank.worldbank.org/source/doing-business

World Bank (2020b) 'Human capital index (HCI)', *World development indicators*. Available at: https://databank.worldbank.org/source/world-development-indicators

World Bank (2021) *Country policy and institutional assessment (CPIA)*. World Bank Group. Available at: https://databank.worldbank.org/source/country-policy-and-institutional-assessment#

World Bank (2022) *GovTech maturity index (GTMI)* (Version 15). Available at: https://datacatalog.worldbank.org/int/search/dataset/0037889/govtech-dataset

World Bank (2023) *The World Bank in DRC – Overview*. Available at: https://www.worldbank.org/en/country/drc/overview

World Customs Organization (WCO) (2003) The Revised Arusha Declaration. Declaration of the Customs Co-Operation Council concerning Good Governance and Integrity in Customs. Brussels: WCO.

CHAPTER 3

The Role of Governments in Improving Domestic Revenue Mobilization

3.1. Introduction

African countries have embarked on a transformative journey of fiscal reform, displaying a renewed determination to bolster their fiscal capacity through efforts to boost domestic revenue mobilization. For decades aid has been pivotal to SSA government revenues. The 1970s and 1980s witnessed an unparalleled increase in total aid to sub-Saharan Africa, surging from less than 12 percent of the region's GDP in 1980 to almost 19 percent in 1994 (Moore, Prichard and Fjeldstad, 2018a; Segura-Ubiergo et al., 2018). Since the 2000s, a significant shift has emerged, with the proportion of aid ranging between 20 percent and 25 percent of government revenues (Tefera and Odhiambo, 2022). While development aid still constitutes a significant portion of government resources, despite a slight decline in the amount transferred to African countries,[46] the past decade has seen a notable shift. Governments are now firmly focusing on strengthening their revenue mobilization systems by making significant strides to increase their tax-to-GDP ratios and mobilize sufficient revenues to finance infrastructure and the provision of public services. The continent is undergoing a new tax era characterized by tax reforms and a significant increase in the proportion of tax revenue in total state revenues, coupled with the importance political elites attach to domestic revenue mobilization (Moore, Prichard and Fjeldstad, 2018b). While direct and indirect taxes form the backbone of revenue generation, non-tax revenues contribute

---

46 Development aid to Africa has experienced a decline in recent years in sub-Saharan Africa. Although official development assistance (ODA) reached record levels in 2022, the overall aid to developing countries has decreased by 2 percent (approximately US$4 billion), affecting over 70 developing countries, including many in Africa (UNCTAD, 2024). Development aid to the least developed countries also saw a 4 percent decline, following an 8 percent decrease the previous year (UNCTAD, 2024). Additionally, the proportion of aid explicitly directed to African countries is at its lowest point in over two decades, with only 25.6 percent of global ODA going to the continent (Harcourt, 2024). This trend is partly due to a shift in donor priorities, including significant increases in aid to Ukraine and other emerging crises (Harcourt, 2024).

to total overall government revenues at a small margin (6.8 percent of GDP) (OECD, AUC and ATAF, 2022).

Recent progress in revenue mobilization could be attributed to several factors – tax policy reforms, strengthening tax administration, digitalization, international support, and political will – propelled by economic growth enjoyed by several countries in recent years (ATAF, 2021). This has catalyzed expansion of tax bases and increased revenue generation. Concurrently, the simplification of tax codes and the modernization of tax systems, coupled with efforts to strengthen the capacity of tax administrations and encourage tax compliance, contributed to reducing tax evasion and avoidance (Segura-Ubiergo *et al.*, 2018; Jacquemot and Raffinot, 2018). Notwithstanding these gains, performance in terms of tax-to-GDP ratio is still lower than Latin American countries and higher-income countries, averaging 17 percent in Africa in 2019 (OECD, AUC, and ATAF, 2022; Segura-Ubiergo *et al.*, 2018). The International Monetary Fund (IMF) estimates that the median country in Africa could increase its tax-to-GDP ratio by about 3 to 5 percent (Segura-Ubiergo *et al.*, 2018). This untapped revenue potential is particularly vast in countries like Nigeria, Madagascar, Cameroon, Congo, Ghana, Gabon, and Togo, thus reflecting the need for governments to implement measures to reduce this revenue gap (Jacquemot and Raffinot, 2018).

This chapter examines the role of governance in boosting domestic revenue mobilization. Domestic revenue mobilization varies significantly across countries and includes, but is not limited to, the mobilization of tax and non-tax revenues, royalties from natural resources, customs and duties, remittances, aid, and grants. This analysis adopts a narrow approach to examining government efforts to generate tax and non-tax revenues, excluding those from the extractive sector but including revenues from state-owned enterprises (SOEs).[47] Although improving revenue systems requires significant investments in technical capacities, the success of these efforts hinges primarily on the commitment of key government actors and political elites to design and support the implementation of sustainable, progressive and equitable tax systems, enact effective tax policies, and strengthen revenue administrations.

The analysis focuses particularly on recent efforts undertaken by Senegal, Cameroon, and Ghana to mobilize tax and non-tax revenues by examining the role of government in the following areas: (1) the design of tax infrastructures, tax incentive regimes and their impact on revenue mobilization and efforts to harness the revenue potential of property-related taxes and high-net-worth

---

47 The analysis excludes revenue mobilization efforts from the extractive sector as well as custom taxes and duties. While these are significant revenue sources, they face distinct and complex challenges that require detailed political and institutional analysis.

individuals; (2) the design and implementation of policy and national strategies to widen the revenue base and improve revenue performance; (3) initiatives engineered to instill optimal governance in SOEs, in order to infuse them with the potential to substantively contribute to domestic revenue generation.

The analysis underlines that policymakers and government elites recognize the importance of boosting domestic revenue mobilization as evidenced by incremental reforms in key taxation areas, as is the case in Cameroon, or through comprehensive reforms that resonate with overarching national priorities aimed at reviving economic and social development as illustrated by Senegal and Ghana. Concurrently, the analysis shows that efforts remain suboptimal concerning overly generous tax incentives, and strategies to tap into property tax revenues and the taxation of high-net-worth individuals. Additionally, despite the recognition that SOEs drain government resources, reforms, and strategies to improve the governance of these companies have been mixed. The chapter emphasizes that while progress has been made, it is not uniform across the countries studied, necessitating more strategies to spur efficient and equitable domestic revenue mobilization systems.

The subsequent sections of this chapter are structured as follows: section 2 provides a concise conceptual exploration of the role of key government and political elites in domestic revenue mobilization reforms and an overview of domestic revenue mobilization performance in Senegal, Cameroon, and Ghana. This section underlines the prevailing trend that governments rely more on indirect tax revenues, with moderate contributions from direct taxes. Additionally, the section highlights the contribution of VAT to indirect tax revenues, outlines revenue losses stemming from tax exemptions, and underscores the potential of taxing properties and high-net-worth individuals. Section 3 sheds light on recent reform programs and efforts implemented in the three countries to strengthen revenue mobilization systems and identifies areas for further improvement. Section 4 analyses the contribution of the three countries' SOEs to domestic revenue mobilization and governmental efforts to render these enterprises more lucrative. The final section presents the conclusion and main takeaways from the three countries, notably the challenges in balancing revenue generation with supporting vulnerable populations, as well as the need to ensure effective governance and public service delivery to foster trust and compliance.

3.2. The politics of domestic revenue mobilization

Domestic revenue mobilization in SSA has long been considered the domain of technical experts, with strategies modeled around a technocratic approach and requiring significant investments and resources to build the technical capacity of tax administrations (Prichard, 2019). This approach was rooted in the conviction that the key constraint on improved performance was the poor design of these systems and weak capacity – and that 'better' policy and development of capacity (i.e., human resources, technologies, or technical capabilities) could strengthen tax systems and increase domestic revenue mobilization. However, technical solutions have yielded modest and unsustainable gains, as evidenced by the slow progress in domestic revenue mobilization performance in several SSA countries, pervasive informality in taxation, weak tax administrations and the proliferation of tax exemptions (Moore, Prichard and Fjeldstad 2018b; Prichard, 2019). A growing agreement is emerging that the key drivers of effective and enhanced domestic revenue mobilization reside in the realm of politics, underlining the pivotal role and commitment of government and political elites in initiating reform and support efforts to boost revenue mobilization (Prichard, 2019; Di John, 2006; Nyirakamana, 2021; Segura-Ubiergo et al., 2018). Robust commitment from the government is undeniably central, especially considering that domestic revenue mobilization requires the extraction of revenue often from segments of society with significant political influence (Prichard, 2019; Nyirakamana, 2021; Cheeseman and Burbidge, 2016; Slemrod, 1990). Indeed, recent successes in revenue mobilization reforms show that they were the result of political processes and are likely to encounter resistance from entrenched interests (Segura-Ubiergo et al., 2018).

The role of the government manifests in multifaceted dimensions. This encompasses but is not restricted to the formulation of appropriate policies and the design of a taxation system that fosters efficiency, progressiveness, and equity. It also involves a careful equilibrium of tax incentives in specific sectors, along with intensified taxation in others. The implementation of sound reform strategies to build efficient revenue administration systems further characterizes the role of government elites in domestic revenue mobilization. Beyond their involvement in policy design, governing elites exercise a pivotal influence in building the capacities of revenue administration and implementing measures to combat tax evasion and corruption while sustaining the momentum and durability of reforms (Prichard, 2019; Moore, Prichard and Fjeldstad 2018b; Segura-Ubiergo et al., 2018). Without unwavering political support, reform endeavors are likely to yield meaningless outcomes. Conversely, with substantial political backing, tax administrations can achieve notable advancements (Moore, Prichard and Fjeldstad, 2018b).

Undoubtedly, across several SSA countries, the design of tax systems has been a complex process resulting from the legacy of colonization, historical processes that followed independence and reforms have been the product of pressure from international financial institutions. Yet, the evolution of these systems over time has been the result of struggles between government elites and the capacity to bring innovation or support efforts for better administration in line with national economic and social development priorities. In the same vein, the evolution of revenue mobilization systems in Senegal, Cameroon and Ghana has indeed been shaped by international pressures. Yet, they have been significantly molded by political decisions. The subsequent sections delve into key governmental efforts aimed at designing taxation systems and supporting revenue mobilization activities. However, before delving into an analysis of recent reforms implemented in the three countries, the upcoming sections present an overview of the performance of both tax and non-tax revenue mobilization. This assessment is compared with the broader regional average for contextual considerations.

3.2.1. Revenue performance in Senegal, Cameroon and Ghana

In the past decade, the pursuit of enhanced fiscal stability through the augmentation of tax and non-tax revenues, measured as a percentage of GDP, has gained traction across various SSA countries. This drive aligns with their medium-term revenue strategies and international commitments.[48] This section provides an overview of these performances based on the most recent available data from 2020. Likewise, these data should be interpreted cautiously as the performances were significantly affected by the Covid-19 crisis. While the tax-to-GDP ratio in Seychelles and South Africa, the highest performers in Africa, exceeded 25 percent in 2020 (OECD, AUC and ATAF, 2022), the trend in tax revenue mobilization in Senegal, Cameroon, and Ghana presents challenges in achieving similar levels, as explained in the paragraphs below.

- **Senegal:** The mobilization of tax revenues in Senegal surpassed the regional average with a tax-to-GDP ratio of 18.1 percent in 2020 (OECD, AUC and ATAF, 2022). Yet, the share of non-tax revenues to GDP ratio stands at 3.4 percent, falling below the regional average of 6.8 percent (OECD, ATAF and CUA, 2022b). In 2020, the mobilization of tax and non-tax revenues amounted to XOF2 518.9 billion (≈US$6 million) against XOF2 546.4 billion (≈US$5.8 million) in 2019, representing a marginal decrease of 1 percent (République du Sénégal, 2021). This performance can be attributed to increases in VAT, income taxes, profits, capital gains, and other tax revenue streams. In particular, the contribution of VAT (32 percent of all tax

---

48 This information is mentioned in the various financial reports of the three countries, including the Medium-Term Revenue Mobilization Strategy in the case of Senegal and the Medium Development Plan for Ghana.

revenues) is above the regional average of 28 percent of the contribution to total tax revenues (OECD, AUC and ATAF, 2022).

- **Cameroon:** In contrast, performance in the mobilization of tax revenues in Cameroon averaged a 12.8 percent tax-to-GDP ratio in 2020, below Senegal and the regional average. This represents a decrease of 1.1 percent compared to 2019 (OECD, AUC and ATAF, 2022). Non-tax revenues accounted for approximately 2.3 percent of GDP, slightly lower than Senegal and below the African average (OECD, AUC and ATAF, 2022). Like Senegal, VAT stands as the main source of revenue, amounting to 31 percent of tax revenues, followed by taxes on goods and services other than VAT, which make up 27 percent and other taxes (including income taxes), representing a share of 18 percent (OECD, ATAF and CUA, 2022b). Tax revenues represent 61.7 percent of the state's own resources and contributed 39.2 percent of the state budget in 2020 (République du Cameroun, 2020). These revenues went from XAF2 932 billion in 2019 (≈US$4.98 million) to XAF2 749.3 billion (≈US$4.94 million)[49] in 2020.[50] This slight decrease could also be explained by the effect of the Covid-19 pandemic crisis on the economy.[51]

- **Ghana:** The performance in tax revenue mobilization improved by 1.5 percent from 2019 to reach 13.4 percent of GDP in 2020 (OECD, AUC and ATAF, 2022a). While this progress surpasses Cameroon's performance, it is below Senegal's achievement. Like Senegal and Cameroon, this perform-ance is lower than the African average of 16 percent. Additionally, Ghana's tax revenue collections were relatively low compared to countries with an equivalent income level worldwide. Notably, taxes on goods and services contribute 26 percent, while VAT constitutes 25 percent of total revenues. Non-tax revenues accounted for 2.8 percent of GDP, also below the African average. In 2019, tax revenue mobilization reached GHC40 595 million (≈US$7.8 million), against a target of GHC44 986 million, representing an outcome of about 90 percent compared to revenue targets (Republic of Ghana, 2021). In 2020, performance was GHC42 405 million (≈US$7.36 million), considered a slight increase of 5 percent compared to 2019.[52]

---

49 Conversion done using this website for 2019 and 2020 rates: https://www.xe.com/currencycharts/?from=XAF&to= USD&view=10Y
50 République du Cameroun, p. 7 of the *Rapport d'exécution Du Budget de l'État Pour l'Exercice 2020*.
51 In 2022 tax revenues exceeded XAF2 000 billion for the first time in Cameroon (Mbodiam, 2022).
52 Conversion was done using this website for 2019 and 2020 rates: https://www.xe.com/currencycharts/?from= GHS&to=USD&view=10Y

Figure 22: Senegal, Cameroon and Ghana revenue mobilization trends in 2015–2020, percent of GDP

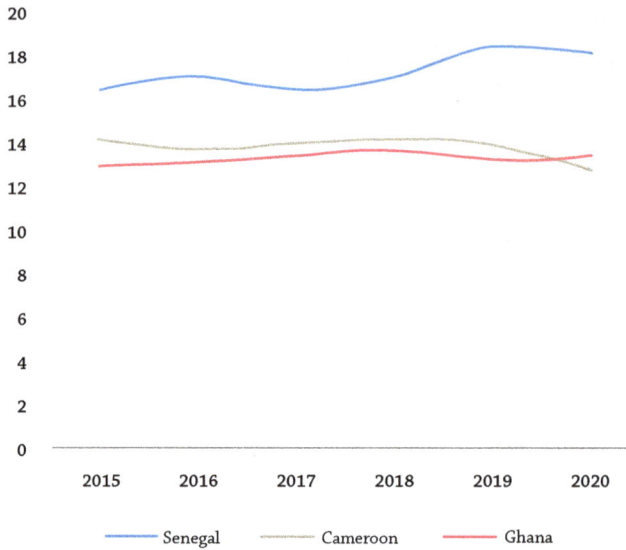

Source: Revenue Statistics in Africa (OECD and ATAF, 2022)

This comparative analysis underscores that the enhanced domestic revenue performance pursued in Senegal, Cameroon, and Ghana has experienced diverse trajectories. It also demonstrates that Senegal shows a comparatively stronger tax revenue mobilization than Ghana and Cameroon. Looking at Figure 22, Senegal's revenue performance increased from 2017 but witnessed a slight decline in 2020. Likewise, the portion of revenues collected as a percentage of GDP has been rising, notably between 2016 and 2018 in Cameroon and Ghana. At the same time, the patterns of tax mobilization performance over time are similar in Ghana and Cameroon, with a marginal increase in performance between 2017 and 2018, followed by a decrease from 2019 to 2020.

This variance can be attributed to an array of factors, including economic fluctuations, disruptions in international trade and investment, and decreased commodity prices and the Covid-19 pandemic (Segura-Ubiergo et al., 2018). The disruptions from the pandemic and ensuing crises were felt in taxes on goods and services, which declined more than taxes on income or other taxes, such as social security contributions and property taxes (OECD, AUC and ATAF, 2022). During the pandemic, the most significant decrease in tax revenues as a share of GDP was VAT, which declined by 0.3 percent on average (OECD, ATAF and CUA,

2022b). Thus, as these countries navigate their revenue strategies and seek to meet international benchmarks, their paths are marked by distinct challenges.

3.2.2. The tax structure in Senegal, Cameroon and Ghana

As SSA countries strive for strong fiscal capacity, the mobilization of tax and non-tax revenues emerges as a pivotal means to achieve this goal. An effective and efficient revenue system not only requires simplicity, efficiency and equity but also aligns with the principles of fairness in the distribution of wealth and income and progressivity. Within this context, the tax structure assumes a key importance, shaping the revenue extraction methods. This section delves into the tax systems of Senegal, Cameroon, and Ghana, assessing the extent to which revenues are raised more progressively or regressively.

The concept of progressivity within a tax system revolves around the fundamental principle that individuals with higher incomes should bear a proportionally greater tax burden compared to those with lower incomes (Suits, 1977). While evaluating the degree of progressivity calls for an in-depth assessment of the entire spectrum of taxes within each country, this chapter employs a narrow approach, focusing on a simplified analysis that involves comparing the relative contributions of direct and indirect taxes to overall domestic revenues.

The consensus among tax experts underscores that an emphasis on indirect taxation can potentially tilt a tax system towards regressivity (OECD, 2018). This assumption stems from the fact that indirect taxes are commonly levied at a fixed percentage rate on the prices of goods and services. Consequently, this structure places a disproportionate tax burden on individuals with lower incomes (Moore, 2015; Decoster et al., 2010). And, because low-income earners typically spend a higher proportion of their income on basic necessities, like food and housing, they spend a more significant proportion of their income on indirect taxes than high-income earners (Moore, Prichard and Fjeldstad, 2018a; Francis, 2021). In contrast, relying on direct taxation, exemplified by income tax, holds the promise of progressivity. Such taxes can be intentionally designed to follow a progressive path, wherein individuals with higher incomes contribute a larger proportion of their earnings to taxes. This not only functions as a mechanism to mitigate income inequality but also ensures a more equitable distribution of the tax burden across various income groups. A combination of direct and indirect taxation captures the careful balance that governments attempt to strike in pursuit of a fair and effective tax system.

Income tax systems in Senegal, Cameroon and Ghana exemplify progressivity because the tax increases in relation to income level. In Senegal, the income tax system is divided across six tax brackets, with the highest bracket taxed at a rate of 40 percent. Personal income tax in Cameroon and Ghana is distributed across four tax brackets ranging from 0 percent to 35 percent. Among the three countries, corporate income tax (CIT) is the highest in Cameroon, reaching 33 percent. Senegal's CIT is calculated at 30 percent, while Ghana imposes only 25 percent, which is lower compared to the other two countries (Trading Economics, n.d.).

Although assessing the fairness of CIT also requires understanding the incidence of these taxes, one can imply that these various rates in the three countries underline some measures of progressivity and equity on basic principles, with the different rates aiming to ensure both horizontal and vertical equity. In terms of horizontal equity, if similar corporations in each country are taxed at these rates, it suggests an attempt to create a level playing field within each national context. Additionally, higher CIT rates might be viewed as a way to tax more profitable entities at a higher rate, assuming that profits are correlated with the ability to pay.

Nonetheless, indirect taxes contribute to a higher percentage of tax revenues than direct taxes in the three countries, increasing the tax systems' degree of regressivity.[53] For instance, in Ghana, 57 percent of tax revenues have been derived from indirect taxes over the past ten years.[54] This is in contrast with countries like South Africa, which enjoy a more progressive system due to their reliance on income, profits, and capital gains to generate over 60 percent of their tax revenues.[55]

Figure 23: Distribution of tax revenues in Senegal, Cameroon and Ghana in 2020

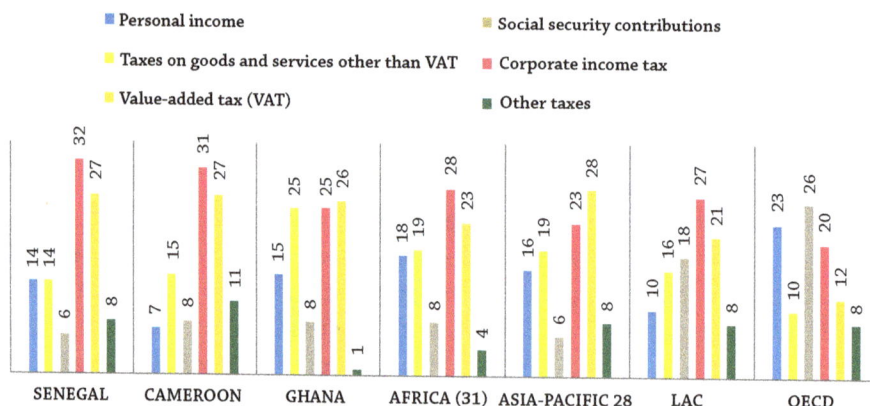

Source: OECD, AUC, ATAF (2022)

---

53 Moore, Prichard and Fjeldstad (2018b) *Taxing Africa: Coercion, Reform and Development*. In addition to the VAT, the most important indirect taxes in Ghana are (1) the Communication Services Tax at 5 percent; (2) the GETFUND Levy at 2.5 percent; (3) the National Health Insurance Levy at 2.5 percent; (4) the Excise Duty at various rates, e.g., the 47.5 percent excise duty on beer; (5) Covid-19 Levy at 1 percent; and (6) import duties at various rates.
54 Francis (2021); Andoh and Nkrumah (2022).
55 OECD, AUC and ATAF (2022).

Central to the dominance of indirect taxes is the VAT, which provided the highest contribution in 2020. In Senegal and Cameroon, VAT contributed significantly to overall tax revenues, with respective shares of 32 percent and 31 percent. In Ghana, however, revenues from VAT accounted for 25 percent of all tax revenues, just after taxes on goods and services other than VAT. To illuminate this trend, Figure 23 offers a glimpse into the distribution of tax revenues across the three countries in 2020.

3.2.2.1 The prominence of the value-added tax

The introduction of VAT is one of the major tax reforms implemented by many SSA countries. This reform was spurred, in part, by the IMF's recommendation to replace prevailing sales and turnover taxes with the VAT framework (Moore, Prichard and Fjeldstad, 2018b). The guiding notion was that the incremental revenues from VAT would stand as a viable substitute for the revenue decline resulting from the reduction of trade taxes. Beyond revenue considerations, the inception of VAT was accompanied by the plan to curtail the phenomenon of "tax cascading" – a scenario where taxes are levied on previous tax payments within the supply chain (Segura-Ubiergo *et al.*, 2018). However, despite the initial success of VAT in fostering a transitional shift in taxation paradigms, experts agree that certain shortcomings persist. These include a reduced tax base, the existence of multiple tax rates, and an elevated standard rate. This underscores the fact that VAT systems, albeit effective in certain dimensions, grapple with the challenge of achieving higher revenue mobilization.

Senegal and Cameroon introduced the VAT, respectively, in 1980 and 1999. The rate in Cameroon is 19.5 percent, and in Senegal, 18 percent – all considered among the highest in Africa (MINFI, 2020). Interestingly, the VAT regime in Ghana underwent several changes as part of the government's discretionary measures to, among other reasons, boost revenue mobilization. The country adopted this tax in 1995 but repealed it mainly due to its high rate (17.5 percent), pressure from businesses to get exemptions and issues with poor record keeping by businesses. The tax was then re-implemented in 1998 at 12.5 percent (Assibey-Mensah, 1999). In 2022, it was again increased to 15 percent as part of the country's measures to earn more revenue amid the economic crisis it is experiencing (GRA, n.d.).[56]

Despite its importance and several discretionary reforms in a bid to generate as much revenue as possible in Ghana, the trends show that VAT's contribution

---

56 The government plans to use this extra revenue for road infrastructure and digitalization.

to total tax revenue has consistently remained below 30 percent over the past fifteen years (Andoh, 2017). Thus, according to Andoh (2017: p. 258), "the much-celebrated VAT may either be reaching the limit of its taxable capacity or the collection effort to convert the available capacity into actual revenue is low". While VAT has undoubtedly contributed to reshaping tax systems, it concurrently serves as a reminder of the challenges inherent in adopting new tax regimes that may be moderately adapted to the contexts in which they are implemented. Similarly, the growing trend towards more regressive taxation in Africa, in Senegal, Cameroon and Ghana, is evidenced by the history of the VAT reforms which has mainly stemmed from, among other factors, international pressures to reform tax systems. Also, despite the limited revenue potential of regressive taxes, including VAT, most tax regimes tend to be regressive. What is the potential explanation for this trend?

While an exhaustive answer would inherently derive from extensive interviews and discussions with political leaders and decision-makers, a prevailing notion underscores the dominance of indirect taxes. These taxes are perceived as conventional and convenient avenues for revenue generation, particularly during times when governments require additional revenues more urgently (IMF, 2011). Furthermore, their relatively easy implementation is coupled with reduced resistance from taxpayers, rendering them a seemingly pragmatic choice for governments. Consequently, the overreliance on such taxes becomes primarily a matter of political strategy. The growing tendency toward increasingly regressive taxation in Africa, specifically in Senegal, Cameroon, and Ghana, can be discernible through the lens of historical VAT reforms and through adoption of regressive taxes or increasing the rates of existing ones.

Nonetheless, a consensus is gradually forming among researchers, policy-makers, and experts, accentuating the potential for alternative revenue streams. The turn towards reviewing tax exemption regimes, given their perverse effect on revenue generation, generating more revenues from direct taxes, encompassing property taxes and the extension of personal income taxation to encompass high-net-worth individuals (HNWIs), emerges as a potential approach to domestic revenue mobilization (Segura-Ubiergo et al., 2018; Moore, Prichard and Fjeldstad, 2018a; Baafi, 2022; Jacquemot and Raffinot, 2018). This change of strategy could yield substantial revenue progressively, equitably and fairly. In this context, the subsequent section examines the impacts of tax exemption systems while also surveying the potential revenue gains emerging from property taxes and high-net-worth individuals.

3.2.2.2. *The perverse effects of tax exemptions on domestic revenue mobilization*

A prominent feature of various tax systems involves the incorporation of tax exemption regimes encompassing "measures directed at investors that provide more favorable tax treatment of certain activities or sectors compared with that available to the general industry" (Moore, Prichard and Fjeldstad, 2018a, p. 134). These include tax holidays, special economic zones, investment credits, etc. Fundamentally, these exemptions can serve as essential incentives to stimulate investment in specific sectors. However, these exemptions, as suggested by numerous experts, can result in diminished revenue generation (Zeng, 2015; Moore, 2015; Jacquemot and Raffinot, 2018). Additionally, it remains widely recognized that exemptions are multiple and are usually granted under conditions that are less transparent, which contributes to eroding the credibility of the tax system (Moore, Prichard and Fjeldstad, 2018b; Jacquemot and Raffinot, 2018; Cheeseman and Burbidge, 2016). Exemptions are frequently disproportionately allocated for political motivations, notably as rewards for political allies to garner support, finance election campaigns, and achieve similar political objectives. Politicians may also find it attractive to introduce new tax incentives to reveal their proactive stance in addressing weak economic performance or to favor some regions. Once established, these exemptions are often difficult to eliminate because they create vested interests among businesses and within the government, even when they are ineffective (Moe, 2005).

While accurately assessing the cost of exemptions in SSA countries is difficult due to limited publicly available data, several governments have recently started publishing tax expenditure reports which list the amounts of exemptions granted and their impact on domestic revenue mobilization. These reports fulfil their regional and international obligations and serve as effective tools for promoting good governance practices.[57] Available data for Senegal, Cameroon, and Ghana provide a reasonable picture of the amount of revenue forgone because of tax exemptions. Existing reports assess these tax expenditures using a simplified method recommended by the West African Monetary and Economic Union (WAMEU). This method involves an estimation of the revenue shortfall that would have been avoided had the tax exemptions or rate reductions not been implemented.

- **Senegal** estimates tax expenditures into two categories: the ordinary law regime (*régime de droit commun*) and the exemption regimes for tax exemptions granted to companies and under special international agreements. The

---

57 The publication of these reports marks a noteworthy step towards a more accurate estimation of exemption costs. However, the process of assessing these tax expenditures varies significantly across countries, posing a challenge in achieving an accurate evaluation. The difficulty lies in the distinct methodologies adopted and the inherent complexities associated with obtaining comprehensive data both within and across nations, as well as within diverse sectors.

report on tax expenditures highlights that in 2020 the country lost XOF846 billion (≈US$1.5 billion) to exemptions, mainly stemming from an increase in tax expenditures related to exemption regimes which reached XOF128 billion in 2020 (Ministère des Finances et du Budget, 2020). This amount represents a 30 percent increase over the span of five years. The report underscores that households were the primary recipients of these tax exemptions, accounting for as much as 45.8 percent of the benefits, followed by businesses at 24.27 percent. Although the report does not explicitly identify the specific companies benefiting the most from these exemptions, an earlier release from the Minister of Industry and Mines revealed that the country experienced a loss of XOF400 billion in revenue from the mining sector during the early 2000s due to tax and customs exemptions. The revenue forgone over these years sheds light on the prolonged negative impact of these exemptions on domestic revenue mobilization.

- Similar to Senegal, exemptions in **Cameroon** are divided into two categories – the ordinary law regime (*régime de droit commun*) and the exemption regimes, both of which continue to remain a significant budgetary concern. The tax expenditure report from 2019 underscores a contrast in comparison to Senegal, with a notable divergence in the distribution of the main beneficiaries of these exemptions. While households are the main beneficiaries in Senegal, companies benefit a substantial 73.9 percent from exemptions in Cameroon, while 26.1 percent are allocated to households. The report pinpoints that in 2019, the agri-food sector benefited the most from these exemptions, closely followed by the mining sector, constituting 18.2 percent and 17.9 percent, respectively, of the tax expenditures (Ministère des Finances, 2019).[58] In a parallel assessment conducted in 2015, a comprehensive analysis revealed a substantial XAF850 billion decrease in revenue for Cameroon, directly attributed to tax exemptions within the extractive and oil sectors (Publish What you Pay, 2018). In 2020, these exemptions were estimated at XAF452.272 billion (≈US$768 million) (Cameroun Actuel, 2023). This amount represents a decrease compared to the costs of exemptions in 2019 which reached XAF584.7 billion (≈US$993 million). The potential explanation for this reduction can be attributed to a presidential directive issued and aimed at curtailing tax expenditures to roughly XAF445 billion in 2020. Despite not fully achieving this target, a decrease of 22 percent in these expenditures was realized during that year.

- Comparable to the scenarios faced by Senegal and Cameroon, **Ghana** confronted notable revenue challenges as the country saw its tax expenditure reaching approximately GHS514 million in 2020 (≈US$87 million). A quick

---

58 A breakdown of who benefited the most from these exemptions in 2020 is not publicly available.

analysis of the trend in Ghana shows that this amount is lower compared to the cost of exemptions in 2021 which was GHS4.85 billion (≈US$921 million) in 2019, or a noteworthy increase of GHS7.43 billion (≈US$1.3 billion) in 2021 (GTED, 2021). Furthermore, in 2022, Ghana's Minister of Finance revealed a loss of around GHS27 billion (≈ US$4 billion) due to tax exemptions granted to some businesses between 2008 to 2020 (Agyeman, 2022). A considerable portion of these expenditures were incurred in the context of the Ghana Free Zones Scheme, which was initiated in 1995 with the primary objective of fostering processing and manufacturing activities through the establishment of export processing zones (EPZs). The scheme opened the entirety of the nation to prospective investors who are afforded the opportunity to leverage the free zones as a platform for generating export-oriented goods and services. The scheme provides benefits, accompanied by a list of tax exemptions, to participating companies.

Table 4. Summary of tax exemptions, key sectors and revenue loss

Country	Year	Tax exemptions (Currency)	Tax exemptions (US$)	Main beneficiaries	Key sectors benefiting	Notable revenue loss (Currency)	Notable revenue loss (US$)
Senegal	2020	XOF846 bn	~US$1.5 bn	Households (45.8%), Businesses (24.27%)	Not specified	XOF400 bn (early 2000s)	-
Cameroon	2019	XAF584.7 bn	~US$993 m	Companies (73.9%), Households (26.1%)	Agri-food (18.2%), Mining (17.9%)	XAF850 bn (2015)	-
Cameroon	2020	XAF452.272 bn	~US$768 m	-	-	-	-
Ghana	2020	GHS514 m	~US$87 m	-	-	GHS27 bn (2008–2020)	~US$4 bn
Ghana	2021	GHS4.85 bn	~US$921 m	-	-	-	-
Ghana	2021	GHS7.43 bn	~US$1.3 bn	-	-	-	-

Sources: Senegal: Rapport d'évaluation des dépenses fiscales, Sénégal (Ministère des Finances et du Budget, 2020). Cameroon: Reports from the Ministry of Finance and other reports from other sources (Ministère des Finances, 2019; Publish What you Pay, 2018; Cameroun Actuel, 2023). Ghana: Global tax expenditure data – Ghana, and newspaper story (GTED, 2021; Agyeman, 2022). Notes: The figures for Senegal and Cameroon include both the ordinary and derogatory regimes of tax exemptions. For Ghana, the figures for 2021 reflect different data points from the same year. The data on notable revenue losses in Ghana spans a longer period (2008–2020) and is not directly comparable to annual figures for other countries.

A common thread is evident when examining exemptions in the three countries and, more broadly, across Africa. First, governments across SSA have extended tax exemptions and incentives with the aim of stimulating economic growth, attracting foreign investment, and supporting specific industries. Nonetheless, striking the right balance between providing tax incentives and ensuring substantial revenue generation remains a complex challenge. Reports highlight a prevailing concern that these exemptions have reached excessive levels, perpetuating revenue deficits that ultimately overshadow the benefits reaped by governments. This is particularly the case for Ghana's Free Zone Scheme, where the advantages, notably in job creation, are lower than the level of exportation expected or even the benefits in terms of exemptions provided to corporations (Nyarko Otoo, 2020).

Second, the tendency to provide substantial tax and other incentives has triggered a disconcerting race to the bottom among countries vying to attract foreign direct investment (FDI). Illustrating this trend, a study by Coulibaly and Camara (2021), examining the mining sector, shows that fluctuations in mining CIT rates have no statistically significant impact on FDI inflows within African economies' gold and silver mining sectors. Similarly, a study conducted by Ali-Nakyea and Amoh (2018) in Ghana questions the efficacy of tax incentives in the natural resource sector, prompting skepticism regarding the direct link between such incentives and FDI flows.

Experts now agree that the ability to attract investments is not invariably correlated with tangible gains. Instead, the attractiveness of the investment climate, including factors like macroeconomic stability, infrastructure quality, and good governance, is often considered in the investor selection process (Ali-Nakyea and Amoh, 2018; Nyarko Otoo, 2020; Tanzi et al., 1981; Abille and Mumuni, 2023). Thus, a growing consensus is that, for those countries continuing to provide more incentives like this despite their limited benefits, the driving force behind this tax competition appears to be primarily rooted in political motives rather than economic rationality (Nyarko Otoo 2020; Moore, Prichard and Fjeldstad, 2018a).

Addressing the revenue shortfall from tax exemptions

Confronted with a significant revenue shortfall, Senegal, Cameroon, and Ghana undertook a series of measures to remedy the situation. These encompassed amendments to their tax codes aimed at enhancing the regulation and oversight of exemption systems and other tax provisions. Additionally, Senegal and Cameroon publish reports on tax expenditures as tools to promote good governance within this domain. These reforms are designed to eliminate specific exemptions or to enhance the monitoring and allocation processes governing these exemptions.

In Ghana, a significant stride was taken with the enactment of the Tax Exemption Bill in 2022, which introduced transparent eligibility criteria for tax exemptions, establishing a framework for strong monitoring, assessment, and enforcement of these exemptions. Notably, the bill established a regulatory mechanism to ensure that granted exemptions serve their intended purposes while simultaneously curbing any abuse of the existing exemption structure.

Furthermore, it fortified the oversight role of the Ministry of Finance in managing exemptions and in preventing abuse (Asiedu, 2022).[59]

Similarly, Cameroon demonstrated proactive commitment in 2019 by eliminating some exemptions. This included the cessation of tax incentives for importing flour and rice, along with the removal of the VAT exemption for life insurance premiums (Barma, 2019). These changes were pivotal components of the 2022–2024 tax policy reform, strategically aligned with the goals of broadening the tax base and fostering economic development.

Table 5. Summary of measures to curb the negative effects of tax exemptions

Country	Year	Measures taken	Details
Senegal	Ongoing	Reporting and regulatory reforms	Publishes reports on tax expenditures to enhance transparency and governance, aiming to eliminate specific exemptions and improve oversight.
Cameroon	2019	Elimination of certain exemptions	Removed tax incentives for importing flour and rice, and VAT exemption for life insurance premiums as part of the 2022–2024 tax policy reform.
Ghana	2022	Enactment of Tax Exemption Bill	Introduced transparent eligibility criteria, a framework for monitoring and enforcement, and strengthened oversight by the Ministry of Finance.

While these reform endeavors are commendable, their true impact remains to be determined. Yet, it is essential to underscore that the success of reforming tax exemption systems hinges on the implementation of strong and effective control measures supported by political actors. Robust political backing is key in overcoming resistance to these reforms and measures, and ensuring taxpayers fulfil their obligations through effective enforcement methods, sustained transparency, and solid commitment.

3.2.2.3. *Exploring alternative revenue sources*

i. Taxing high-net-worth individuals

In seeking to diversify revenue sources and explore alternative avenues for revenue generation, the taxation of high-net-worth individuals (HNWIs) emerges as a promising strategy to enable governments to earn substantial revenue. The underlying premise is that HNWIs possess more resources and can pay a larger

---

59 This bill is part of several measures taken in 2016, when the Ministry of Finance intensified its oversight in an effort to limit the use of special permits that exempt imports from custom duties and VAT and amendment of the process for approving exemptions to include compulsory clearance by the Ministry. However, these previous steps have not had significant enough impacts.

share of their income in taxes without encountering a similar financial burden as low-income individuals (Kangave *et al.*, 2016).

In many African countries, income and wealth inequality remains a significant challenge, with a small percentage of the population owning a disproportionate share of the wealth. Evidence shows that wealthy Africans pay little or no income tax at all, and although the number of African billionaires is few, yet rapidly expanding, many countries have not succeeded in implementing effective systems to tax HNWIs (Dietz, 2023; Moore, Prichard and Fjeldstad, 2018a; Kangave *et al.*, 2016). In Uganda, for example, a study found that although HNWIs were registered with the Uganda Revenue Authority (URA), only a small number paid their income taxes (Kangave *et al.*, 2016). This discrepancy largely stems from enforcement challenges within this specific taxpayer category. Similarly, Nigeria has the third-largest number of individuals with a wealth of at least US\$1 million in Africa, and their private wealth is valued at over half of Nigeria's GDP (Kamer, n.d.). Nevertheless, the country only collects a small portion of potential tax revenues from those individuals (Ademola, Dada and Akintoye, 2019).

Approaches to generating revenues from HNWIs in Ghana, Senegal, and Cameroon show both similarities and differences. First, all three countries have introduced the Taxpayer Identification Number (TIN) system to identify and track taxpayers, with the aim of registering more HNWIs. Second, these countries have been engaged in reviews and updates of their tax legislation to ensure their relevance and efficacy in the taxation of HNWIs. For instance, efforts in the three countries have been directed towards reforming their personal income tax regimes to capture the incomes of high-net-worth individuals who might have previously avoided or evaded their tax responsibilities. More specifically, in 2021, the Ghana Revenue Authority (GRA) proposed changes to the personal income tax regime to capture the incomes of HNWI (persons with approximately US\$1 million in liquid financial assets) who may have previously avoided or evaded taxes (Segbefia, 2021). These changes aimed to address the issue of potential tax avoidance or evasion among this segment. GRA also indicated that it would enforce payments from HNWIs, whose asset base and affluence do not match the tax they pay. To do so, the agency configured and synchronized its data with 14 other government institutions, including the Driver and Vehicle Licensing Authority (DVLA) and the Social Security and National Insurance Trust (SSNIT), to easily identify HNWIs and streamline the process of enforcing tax compliance (Segbefia, 2021). Lastly, Senegal have taken a proactive stance by introducing luxury taxes specifically targeting luxury vehicles. On a parallel note, Cameroon has chosen to implement a tax on higher rental incomes to generate more revenue from this category of taxpayers.

In a nutshell, while approaches to taxing HNWIs share certain fundamental strategies, they also show nuanced distinctions that are reflective of countries' political and legislative priorities. As underscored by the limited yet compelling findings and studies, there is a potential to generate substantial revenue through the taxation of HNWIs. By implementing effective taxation strategies, governments can effectively contribute to the redistribution of a portion of this wealth, thereby helping reduce economic inequality. However, it is important to recognize that while taxes can reduce inequalities, they alone do not necessarily raise the incomes or asset stocks of the poor. The impact of taxes on inequality ultimately depends on how the revenue is spent. Effective redistribution relies on the allocation of tax proceeds in a manner that supports equitable growth and social welfare, which is not automatically guaranteed. Yet, as revenues are increasingly needed for fair redistribution, priority should therefore be given to urgently pursuing initiatives aimed at fortifying administrative infrastructures, and enforcement mechanisms and improving the capacity required to effectively manage this particular taxpayer category.

ii. Tapping into the property tax potential

Property-related taxes (tax on buildings, rental income, stamp duties, land rates, etc.) are also considered an important source of revenue, particularly for governments in Africa. Furthermore, the increasing urbanization and real estate boom in several African cities underlines the immense potential for generating property tax revenues. Although it is agreed that these are *easy* and progressive taxes to collect, they are known to be the most underperforming major tax in Africa, with a performance ranging between 0.1 and around 1 percent of GDP (Slack and Bird, 2014; Fjeldstad, Ali and Goodfellow, 2017; Franzsen and McCluskey, 2017). The reasons for this underperformance are mainly technical. Nonetheless, research evidence has recently pointed to the political resistance to effective property taxation (Jibao and Prichard, 2013; Moore, Prichard and Fjeldstad, 2018a). According to Slack and Bird (2014), property tax is perhaps the most politically sensitive tax because of its direct nature.

Reform initiatives primarily center around the comprehensive identification of taxable properties and overhaul of property valuation systems frequently face resistance from politically connected taxpayers, wealthy property owners and influential economic elites, who are inclined to evade tax obligations or resist progressive reforms that might increase their tax liabilities (Collier *et al.*, 2018; Jibao and Prichard, 2013). Notably, recent instances of successful reform, as witnessed in Freetown, were facilitated by the proactive support of political leadership (Prichard, Kamara and Meriggi, 2020). The following section includes efforts undertaken by the three countries to tap into the property tax potential.

3.3. Recent reform programs implemented to boost tax and non-tax revenues

Government efforts supported by a strong commitment from political leaders are the fundamental pillar of improving domestic revenue mobilization to advance economic development and enhance the living conditions of citizens. Against this background, Senegal, Cameroon, and Ghana have implemented reform programs under their political leadership. These reforms differ in their scale and implementation strategy.

Senegal and Ghana designed comprehensive reform programs aligning with the respective governmental development priorities. In Senegal, the prioritization of domestic revenue mobilization is integrated with a broad program called *Plan Sénégal Émergent (PSE)*, a strategic blueprint aimed at achieving the country's development aspirations by 2035. In parallel, Ghana's domestic revenue mobilization strategy is embodied within the national program Ghana Beyond Aid, an overarching vision with the key objective of reducing the country's reliance on external assistance and aid. Conversely, Cameroon has adopted targeted initiatives to reform specific areas of taxation as part of governmental priorities and commitments to the IMF. Unlike Senegal and Ghana, where revenue mobilization reforms intertwine with their respective national agendas, reforms in Cameroon are primarily a response to the existing economic context and the pursuit of support from financial partners.

This section provides a high-level overview of these reform endeavors. Although a comprehensive analysis tracking the process of these reforms and their impacts over time would provide a more nuanced assessment of the roles played by key political figures in driving change despite potential resistance, the limited space and scope of this chapter only allow for a high-level review of recent reform dynamics to underline the key role of government elites in undertaking and supporting revenue mobilization reforms. Therefore, the analysis is restricted to key aspects indicating reform efforts, including in the area of property taxation, at different periods in each country.

3.3.1. Government strategies to boost domestic revenue mobilization in Senegal, Ghana and Cameroon

3.3.1.1. Plan for an Emerging Senegal (PSE)

Although revenue mobilization efforts have continuously been a government priority, this was further defined as a central component in the *Plan Sénégal Émergent* (PSE – Plan for an Emerging Senegal) program adopted in 2014. This broad development agenda pinpoints the role of political actors in tax reforms, given the investments and resources deployed to support revenue-raising activities. PSE is a 15-year strategic development plan aiming to transform Senegal into an emerging economy. PSE emphasizes structural reforms, infrastructure development, and private sector growth to drive economic diversification and reduce poverty. Its formulation was accompanied by the launching of a vast project of tax reforms to modernize and make the General Tax Code more effective. Key objectives include the increase of tax performance; and broadening the tax base to reach a tax-to-GDP ratio of 20 percent in 2023, which would enable the government to achieve its development projects and fulfil its international commitments in terms of fiscal transition (Gouvernement du Sénégal, 2014). These fiscal reforms were carried out with transparency objectives translated into the adoption, in 2012, of the Code of Transparency in Public Finance Management. This urges the government to publish all information concerning the levels of tax levies and revenue amounts. Additionally, the country obtained membership in the Global Forum on Transparency and Exchange of Information for Tax Purposes as evidence of a strong commitment to adopting international standards and good practices. By joining this forum, the country is subject to peer review.[60]

Revenue mobilization objectives and plans are formulated in the Medium-Term Revenue Mobilization Strategy (SRMT) 2020–2025, led by the Ministry of Finance and operationalized through the *Plan Yaatal,* under the leadership of the Directorate General of Taxation and Domains (DGID). *Yaatal* aims to expand the tax base and promote fiscal citizenship through a simplified legislative system, investment in technology for optimal revenue mobilization, maximum use of information, and land use as a key source of domestic revenue mobilization (DGID, 2020). The driving force in achieving these objectives of the *Yaatal* program comes from top-level government officials, including the former DGID Director General, who, following findings from a survey report produced by the National Agency for Statistics and Demography (ANSD),

---

60 More information is needed to assess the impact of these commitments. Ghana and Cameroon joined the forum, respectively, in 2011 and 2012.

recognized the enormous potential of expanding the revenue base. This statistics report revealed that the country had about half a million economic units/entities. However, only about 85 000 were registered in the DGID databases, and only about 30 percent (25 000 taxpayers) complied with tax payments (ANSD, 2014).

The exploitation of land revenues occupies a prominent place in this agenda. It converges with almost all the main priorities of the current government's agenda, including development, decentralization, land reform and the modernization and digitalization of the administration (République du Sénégal, 2018; OECD, 2019). Like in many countries, property taxes in Senegal perform poorly, despite their revenue potential. Estimates show that performance accounts for 0.4 percent of GDP. In cities like Dakar, which is experiencing growing urbanization and real estate expansion, only 20 percent of eligible taxpayers are included in the database. Of those, only 12 percent of owners paid property taxes in 2018 (Knebelmann, 2019). Harnessing of the property tax revenue is taking place through a vast census program of properties throughout the country, building on previous reforms implemented in the early 2000s.[61] The recent reforms began in 2019 under the financing of several actors, mainly the Government of Senegal, the World Bank, and the French Development Agency. It is expected that the data collected will also enable the DGID to capture a large number of potential taxpayers, in addition to estimating the characteristics and categories of taxpayers in order to adopt the necessary measures and strategies to engage with them. Several achievements have been made, mainly the increase in the number of taxpayers in the DGID databases. So far, the tax-to-GDP ratio performance has increased by about 14 percent in ten years, from 15.9 percent in 2010 to 18.1 percent in 2020 (OECD, AUC and ATAF, 2022). Although these reforms are encountering some difficulties (limited resources, handling large volumes of data, etc.), they underline how government elites can initiate domestic revenue mobilization reforms when these align with their political priorities.

3.3.1.2. Ghana Beyond Aid

In Ghana, key measures to improve tax and non-tax revenue mobilization date back to the 2000s, with the establishment in 2009 of the Ghana Revenue Authority under the supervision of a Board of Directors. These efforts persisted in 2019 as part of the Ghana Beyond Aid program. Prior to the creation of the GRA, "different classes of taxes were administered by three independent

---

61 In 2009, with funding from the African Development Bank, the State of Senegal implemented the Support Program for the Modernization of the Cadastre (PAMOCA). However, despite significant investments, this resulted in a marginal increase in property revenues and limited broadening of the revenue base.

semi-autonomous revenue agencies: the Customs, Excise and Preventive Service (CEPS), the VAT Service (VATS) and the Internal Revenue Service (IRS)" (Moore, Prichard and Fjeldstad, 2018b). It was expected that the harmonization of these activities under the Ghana Revenue Authority (GRA) would lead to a more coherent alignment of revenue mobilization strategies and the modernization of the revenue administration. Since its inception, the GRA has embarked on a series of administrative reforms, embodied in three strategic plans covering the periods of 2012–2014, 2015–2017 and 2018–2021. These strategies are "designed to integrate and fully modernize the Authority to enable it to carry out its mandate, to strengthen enforcement mechanisms, broaden the tax base, improve processes and procedures and implement innovative measures to increase tax revenue collections" (Moore, Prichard and Fjeldstad, 2018a, p. 34).

Like Senegal, where revenue mobilization strategies are integrated into the broader objectives of the PSE, Ghana's recent reforms are reflected in the medium-term development plans adopted every three years. Government commitment to improving domestic revenue mobilization has culminated in a positive progression with the launch in 2019 of the Ghana Beyond Aid program. This program is centered around the principles of self-sufficiency, economic transformation, and sustainable development. Its principal goal is to reduce reliance on external development aid and to achieve self-sustained financing for fundamental sectors such as education, healthcare, sanitation, and water resources (Republic of Ghana, 2019). This program places emphasis on accountable governance, transparency, and prudent resource management, aimed at forging a self-reliant and prosperous Ghana.

Revenue mobilization objectives and measures are articulated in a series of reforms building on revenue mobilization initiatives initiated in the 2000s. These include enhancing the efficiency of revenue collection agencies, particularly the Ghana Revenue Authority, facilitating the efficient identification of potential taxpayers, ensuring robust enforcement of tax payments (especially within the mining sector), curbing corruption, fostering efficiency within state-owned enterprises, and optimizing expenditure and public investments. A notable priority for the Ghana Beyond Aid program is the expansion of the revenue base, with the ultimate ambition of increasing the tax-to-GDP ratio to 18 percent by 2023 and eventually to 23 percent by 2028 (Republic of Ghana, 2019). As emphasized in the reform document, while the country's official voter registry accounts for 15.7 million individuals, merely around 1.2 million are effectively registered for taxation purposes. This divergence between voters and taxpayers highlights a potential for incorporating additional individuals and businesses into the tax net through mechanisms like the national digital address system and the national identification system.

Other revenue mobilization initiatives have been implemented in response to the post-Covid economic crisis. On the one hand, the country adopted new taxes, such as the e-levy, a 1.5 percent tax on electronic fund transfers exceeding GHS100 (around US$6.50) per day, introduced in May 2022. It is estimated that the e-levy "could bring in more revenue as more businesses transit from the informal to the formal sector, thus meeting some of the goals of the levy to broaden the tax base".[62] While more information is needed to assess its impact, the e-levy is considered unfair to the poor, regressive, and less effective in generating revenue from high-potential taxpayers.[63]

On the other hand, the GRA has revived the rental income tax system (also called rent tax), a tax paid on income revenues at a rate of 8 percent for residential properties and 15 percent for commercial properties. The rent tax was levied in 1973, but required, in practice, a higher level of compliance and a strong capacity of the administration to collect more information on rented property and potential taxpayers. Since 2021, several awareness-raising efforts and the implementation of digital payment systems have been put in place to encourage compliance (Effah, 2021). Anecdotal evidence shows that rent tax revenues have increased significantly, and the government is considering implementing a geolocation and identification system for all properties to capture more payers.

Overall, progress has been recorded, particularly evident in the increased tax-to-GDP ratio over time, rising from over 10 percent of GDP in 2010 to 13.4 percent in 2020 (Iddrisu *et al.*, 2021, p. 31). However, this progress for Ghana remains modest in comparison to similarly positioned countries and may present challenges in attaining the targeted 18 percent tax-to-GDP ratio by 2023 (OECD, AUC and ATAF, 2022).

3.3.1.3 *Fragmented strategies for domestic revenue mobilization in Cameroon*

In Cameroon, the government recognizes the mobilization of domestic revenues as an indispensable instrument for economic development. Multiple initiatives have been undertaken to modernize mobilization systems, both in alignment with the government's agenda and in response to pressure from donor entities. This contrasts with Senegal and Ghana, where a comprehensive, long-term revenue mobilization strategy has been formulated by elites, aligning with the government's long-term development and economic advancement objectives.

---

62 Santoro, Abounabhan and Diouf (2022), 'Ghana's new e-levy'.
63 For more on this, see Rogan et al. (2023); Santoro, Abounabhan and Diouf (2022).

Central efforts are directed at tackling three critical challenges: (1) addressing the high burden of tax expenditure; (2) the sizeable informal sector, which, as observed in various African countries, contributes significantly to economic activity but its revenue potential has not yet been fully harnessed; (3) the inadequate individual contribution to revenue mobilization, and the need for strategies and measures to boost individual contributions. These efforts have been implemented alongside the amendment of the Tax Code, which was last updated in 2023.

In the area of the informal sector, the government has taken steps to, among other strategies, strengthen the withholding tax mechanism, which facilitates tax deductions to be made on transactions conducted by informal sector enterprises with large enterprises. This mechanism allowed the government to mobilize over XAF50 billion yearly from the informal sector. Additionally, the traceability of cash transactions has been strengthened – corporate tax deductions for expenses exceeding XAF500 000 and VAT deductions for invoices surpassing XAF100 000 paid in cash have been prohibited. All these actions have increased the taxable population by 58 percent, from 89 741 in 2015 to more than 140 000 professional taxpayers to date. However, other complementary measures remain to be considered, given the capacity of the informal sector to reinvent itself.

Furthermore, like other countries, Cameroon's Directorate General is contemplating additional reforms related to the registration of more taxpayers, particularly targeting those with potential contributions via property taxes. Currently, taxpayers, including those who pay property taxes, must declare their assets to receive tax notices. Nonetheless, the process is complex, thus discouraging a large number of citizens from doing so. In response to this challenge, the Directorate-General of Taxes, or *Direction Générale des Impots* (DGI), has set up Divisional Centers to streamline the process, allowing the digital implementation of the annual assets' declaration of non-professional taxpayers. Yet, efforts to tax property owners are relatively minor compared to that of the Senegalese revenue authority.

Finally, the DGI has developed a three-year plan for 2023–2025 to modernize the Cameroonian tax system, prompted by findings from the Tax Administration Diagnostic Assessment Tool (TADAT) and IMF recommendations. These reforms are broadly oriented towards four main dimensions: (1) increasing tax revenue mobilization; (2) improving the quality of tax services; (3) the establishment of a modern information system at the DGI; (4) the management and coordination of tax services (Djotié, 2022). As this plan is under development, it is still early to assess its impact. Among the three countries studied, Cameroon is the one that represents a slight increase in its tax-to-GDP ratio. This increased by 10.8 percent, from 11.5 percent in 2010 to 12.8 percent in 2020.

Table 6. Summary of recent tax reforms in Senegal, Ghana and Cameroon

Country	Reform initiative	Year	Key measures and details
Senegal	Plan Sénégal Émergent (PSE)	2014 (Adopted)	15-year strategic plan focusing on structural reforms, infrastructure, and private sector growth. Aims for a tax-to-GDP ratio of 20 percent by 2023. Includes transparency reforms and membership in the Global Forum on Transparency and Exchange of Information.
	Medium-Term Revenue Mobilization Strategy (SRMT) 2020–2025	2020	Led by the Ministry of Finance, includes the *Plan Yaatal* to expand the tax base, improve technology, and utilize land revenues. Key reform feature: improving property tax performance through a national property census.
Ghana	Ghana Beyond Aid Program	2019 (Launched)	Aims for self-sufficiency and reduced aid dependency. Focuses on expanding the revenue base, increasing the tax-to-GDP ratio to 18 percent by 2023 and 23 percent by 2028. Includes new taxes like the e-levy and revived rent tax system.
	Tax Exemption Bill	2022	Introduced transparent criteria for tax exemptions, enhanced monitoring and enforcement, and strengthened the oversight role of the Ministry of Finance.
Cameroon	Tax Code Amendments	2023	Updated to address high tax expenditure and informal sector issues. Strengthened withholding tax mechanisms and cash transaction traceability.
	Informal Sector Taxation	Ongoing	Enhanced withholding tax mechanism, prohibited cash deductions over specific thresholds, and increased taxable population by 58 percent.
	Tax Administration Modernization Plan	2023–2025	Three-year plan focusing on increasing tax revenue, improving tax services, establishing a modern information system, and coordinating tax services.

3.3.2. Key insights from Senegal, Ghana and Cameroon reform programs

Key insights can be drawn from these reform endeavors. First, it is evident that progress has been achieved in advancing reforms, leading to an increase in revenue gains over the past two decades. Notably, digitalization has significantly impacted efforts to strengthen revenue mobilization systems in all three countries. This is hardly surprising, given the increasing momentum of information technologies in various African nations since the 2000s due to their transformative potential. Since Chapter 2 provides an in-depth exploration of IT systems, a concise overview of these initiatives is presented here. In Senegal, Cameroon, and Ghana, digitalization plays a key role in reform initiatives. Adopted technologies serve to streamline revenue administration processes, manage tax-related data, facilitate data sharing across different units within tax administrations, and simplify payment processes. Furthermore, digital solutions contributed to tracking revenues, reducing revenue leakages, and ensuring effective enforcement. In harmonizing taxpayer data, all three countries have implemented Taxpayer

Identification Number systems to improve taxpayer identification, maintain accurate databases, and avoid the duplication of taxpayer identities.

Second, the trend in revenue mobilization shows that the three countries rely more on regressive taxes, which are convenient and easy to adopt. The progress in revenue performance has not led to the attainment of high tax-to-GDP ratios envisioned in their reform programs. Furthermore, it becomes clear that governments can earn more revenue by reducing tax incentives and tapping into the revenue potential of progressive taxes. While challenges related to technical capacity and economic conditions have contributed to this mixed revenue performance, the most important challenges are political and accentuate the importance of the support of political and government elites in advancing reforms.

Third, considering that revenue mobilization can potentially be resisted, in particular by influential groups, it is imperative for countries to contemplate strategies for ensuring the cooperation of these influential groups within the tax regime while preserving their privileges and interests from perceived threats posed by reforms. All these efforts require strong political commitment and promises and actions to inform taxpayers that increased revenue mobilization would benefit taxpayers more significantly. This, among other elements, entails firm commitments to review public expenditure and develop strategies to establish stronger links between revenue mobilization and service provision, better governance through transparency in spending, and greater accountability.

The last section provides an overview of the role of SOEs in generating domestic revenues, the difficulties encountered, the impact of their poor performance on public spending and the measures undertaken by governments to improve their governance standards.

3.4. The challenges of state-owned enterprises in contributing to domestic revenue mobilization

State-owned enterprises (SOEs) are expected to play a substantial role in generating domestic revenues in Africa by providing, at a cost, essential goods and services to the citizens on behalf of the government. In many African countries, SOEs are the leading providers of critical infrastructure such as energy, water, and transportation services. Moreover, these enterprises benefit from governmental financial support, as administrations frequently channel subsidies, grants, loans, or guarantees to boost their operational capabilities and ensure the continuity of services. Among the many SOEs in SSA countries, the company Ethiopian Airlines is considered a successful example in terms of expansion and growing revenue generation.[64] However, additional examples of successful SOEs are scarce, and the generalized trend in several African countries is that, despite significant public investments, SOEs continue to face several challenges, including inefficiency, corruption, and mismanagement. It is assumed that public investments tend to create more dependence and reduced incentives to improve their financial performance. All these challenges have affected the ability of SOEs to generate revenues and fulfil their mandates effectively. Moreover, while these state enterprises are generally perceived as draining public funds, thus requiring reforms to enhance their cost-effectiveness, this has been challenging due mainly to political interference.[65] This interference has often led to appointing unqualified and inexperienced individuals to leadership positions or the lack of sanctions for mismanagement.

Several reforms have been implemented to improve SOE revenue generation, the most important being privatization, which involves transferring ownership and control from the government to private investors. Although the impact of privatization on the profitability of SOEs is mixed, it is still deemed one of the strategies to enhance efficiency, promote innovation, and reduce political interference in the management of SOEs. Other reforms have included restructuring and downsizing SOEs to reduce operational costs and improve financial performance by improving corporate governance and enhancing transparency and accountability.[66] Additionally, governments have introduced measures to improve the regulatory environment and promote competition in the sectors where they operate (Olugbade *et al.*, 2021). Indeed, with proper governance, management, and investment, SOEs can play a crucial role in developing and growing African economies. Like in most African countries, the ability of SOEs to generate enough revenues in Senegal, Cameroon, and Ghana has been limited, as they often face challenges related to governance, efficiency, and financial performance.

Senegal: Senegal has more than twenty state-owned companies operating in diverse sectors, including transportation like Air Senegal, water and energy represented by the *Société nationale d'électricité du Sénégal* (Senelec), construction and infrastructure under SN-HLM, as well as the mining sector. The performance of these companies varies from one company to another, but the widespread trend underscores their limited profitability and the continuous dependence on government subsidies to sustain their operations.

More specifically, Air Senegal, launched in 2016 to replace Senegal Airlines and as part of the Plan for an Emerging Senegal to revitalize the tourism sector, received a financial contribution of XOF40 billion from the government

---

64 Andoh *et al.* (2019).
65 Appiah-Kubi (2001); Blunt (1970); Qhobosheane (2018).
66 Mutize and Tefera (2020); Ackers and Adebayo (2022).

(République du Sénégal, 2018, p. 52). However, after more than five years of service, the company is struggling to make these investments profitable. A report published in 2023 indicated that Air Senegal had contracted about XOF22 billion of debt in 2022, 5 years into operation (Fualdes, 2023). Explicit factors contributing to this poor performance are unavailable. However, it is plausible that the challenging business environment inherent to the aviation industry, characterized by intense competition, necessitates exceptional operational excellence and customer service for profitability. In response to this poor performance, a change in leadership was undertaken, accompanied by performance-oriented reforms, resulting in a reduction of losses in revenues of more than 50 percent at the beginning of 2023 (Diallo, 2019). This underscores a concerted effort to address the operational deficiencies and financial challenges that have burdened the enterprise.

Conversely, Senelec, which encountered financial difficulties in addition to losses of billions XOF Francs over the past decade, is undergoing a gradual transformation, now generating revenues that contribute to government income following its comprehensive restructuring (BBC News Afrique, n.d.). There is every reason to believe that government initiatives have allowed Senelec to expand its services through the installation of new power plants and the increase of its penetration rate of up to 64 percent across the country (Ba, 2023). Moreover, all indications point towards a political commitment to enhance the productivity of SOEs deriving from the political leadership, particularly from the current president. The presence of regulatory bodies such as *the Commission de Régulation du Secteur de l'Énergie (CRSE)* (overseeing Senelec operations) also plays a pivotal role in overseeing the governance and operations of these entities. This supervision in turn promotes effective corporate governance and the modernization of activities, including the implementation of information technology systems in order to streamline operations and adapt them to prevailing economic trends. It is worth noting that while certain state-owned enterprises, like Air Senegal, face challenges in achieving profitability, the government's active engagement in reform and enhancement demonstrates its commitment to fostering more sustainable and effective outcomes for SOEs in Senegal.

Cameroon: In Cameroon, about 44 SOEs are subsidized by the State and like in many SSA countries, they continue to generate losses. A 2019 government report indicated that these SOEs experienced 14. 5 percent in losses, representing a 6.5 percentage point reduction from the figures recorded in 2018.[67] These enterprises include the airline, Camair, the national refining company Sonora and the telecommunications company, Camtel. In alignment with its commitments

---

67 Information deriving from the 2021 Finance Law.

to the IMF, the Cameroon Government has agreed to put these companies under performance contracts starting in 2023. However, a study published by Cameroonian researchers in 2022 shows that performance contracts would not be able to boost the governance of Cameroonian public companies, given the inefficiency of boards of directors and external audit bodies and the pervasive political interference (Nga Nga and Ebele Ombede, 2022). Instead, the authors suggest, among other recommendations, strengthening the accounting skills of auditors, strengthening human capacities, limiting the mandates and multiple roles of managers, and reducing political interference in the appointment of managers. It is still early to assess the tangible impact of these performance contracts, but improving the corporate governance of these companies and reducing political interference can certainly be key to increased profitability and sustainability.

Ghana: In Ghana, the 47 SOEs continue to generate losses. However, as part of the Ghana Beyond Aid plan, the government has added the reform of SOEs to its list of priorities. These reforms encompass maintaining and setting targets for the board management of each enterprise, strong oversight of their performance and rewards for good performance and sanctions for poor performance. It is in this reform context that the State Interest and Governance Authority (SIGA) was implemented in 2019 to monitor SOE performance. SIGA is responsible for overseeing the operations and management of SOEs and ensuring that they operate in a financially sustainable and efficient environment. In addition to monitoring and evaluating the performance of SOEs, the agency also provides guidance and support to the boards and management teams of SOEs and facilitates the privatization of non-strategic SOEs. SIGA publishes reports that measure the progress of these companies and rank their performance to encourage more action and adopt strategies to improve their operations. It is estimated that SIGA's efforts have helped reduce SOE losses from 73 percent in 2018 to 49 percent in 2020. Moreover, of the 47 SOEs, at least one company paid a dividend to the state in 2020.

Box 4. Strategies to improve the contributions of Africa's state-owned enterprises to domestic revenue mobilization

In the three countries, despite variations in performance, the overarching tendency points to limited profitability, often necessitating government subsidies to support SOE operations. Yet, key exhaustive points can be taken into consideration in restructuring SOE governance and profitability strategies.

- A comprehensive restructuring promoting better corporate governance and modernization of operations, the implementation of agencies to monitor performance and promoting transparent, accountable, and financially sustainable operations can lead to a reduction in government investment losses. In fact, implementing a performance-based system with indicators, comparing against industry benchmarks, and adjusting strategies based on outcomes could drive continuous improvement and adaptability of SOEs to the constantly changing business environment. Additionally, a performance-based incentive system can further motivate employees and leaders to contribute to productivity gains and customer service, which are key to increasing the competitiveness of these enterprises. A system of incentives can also reward performance and innovation through promotions or recognition of efforts aligned with organizational goals.
- To enhance the financial viability of SOEs, it is imperative to minimize political interference in appointing SOE managers or in conducting operations. Additionally, improving auditing skills and ensuring transparent management and accountability mechanisms can improve the overall governance of SOEs.
- Fostering the capacity of SOE management teams and personnel is essential. Governments should invest in training programs that equip employees with the necessary skills to navigate competitive industries and adapt to technological advancements, thereby enhancing efficiency and service quality.
- As observed in Ghana, with SIGA, or CRSE in Senegal, independent regulatory and oversight bodies can play a crucial role in overseeing SOE activities, promoting fair competition, and ensuring that decisions are driven by economic considerations rather than political interests.

3.5. Conclusion

Domestic revenue mobilization is becoming a priority for many African governments in the context of multiple crises and declining development aid. The concerted efforts and notable advancements made in the past decade towards mobilizing tax and non-tax revenues underscore the significance accorded to revenue mobilization by governments and political elites. The cases of Senegal, Ghana and Cameroon shed light on how these efforts are deployed, particularly as part of national agendas or targeted strategies. Despite mixed results, these reforms have contributed to increased revenue mobilization. Therefore, there is still enormous revenue potential to be harnessed.

While the expansion of the revenue base has primarily involved the integration of more indirect taxation, this has at the same time intensified the regressive nature of the tax systems. To offset this, considerable prospects lie in increasing strategies for more direct taxation, in particular, property-related taxes, the taxation of high-net-worth individuals (HNWIs), and a more rational distribution of exemptions to extract enhanced revenue and limit revenue losses from excessive exemptions. Furthermore, unexplored fiscal opportunities exist, such as levying taxes on the agricultural and informal sectors.

Expanding on the agricultural sector, in particular, can generate substantial revenue if tax regimes are carefully designed so that agricultural production and competition are not impacted. Indeed, one of the challenges is that many smallholder farmers in Africa live on subsistence and may be unable to pay taxes. Furthermore, the agricultural industry is frequently vulnerable to price fluctuations and weather-related concerns, making forecasting revenues complicated. Payments and enforcement may also be difficult because many farmers operate in remote regions, making it harder for tax officials to monitor their activities and ensure tax compliance. Given this complexity, countries aiming to generate more revenues from this sector need to strike a balance between the need to raise revenue and the need to support small-scale farmers and promote food security and the ability to earn a livelihood – and design appropriate policies to achieve these goals.

Similar challenges are reflected in taxing the informal sector, which plays a pivotal role in African economies. While the contribution of the informal sector to revenue remains modest, taxing this sector would require context-based policies taking into account the need for increased revenues, formalization, economic growth, and social equity. Considering that many African countries struggle with incomplete or unreliable economic data due to the prevalence of informal activities, taxation of the informal sector can encourage the maintenance of accurate records on economic activities, leading to more accurate economic indicators and facilitating informed policy decisions.

Nonetheless, the advantages come hand in hand with trade-offs, such as limited short-term revenue gains, disproportionate collection costs vis-à-vis revenues, non-compliance, and the risk of exacerbating poverty. Most informal economic actors earn insufficient incomes, rendering excessive taxation a burden that could further marginalize vulnerable populations and amplify poverty, especially for women.

Considering this latent potential, governments still have to put in more effort. At the same time, expanding the revenue base and increasing the tax burdens more progressively and equitably should be complemented by effective governance of public funds. Across the continent, the provision of public services has been inadequate and unsatisfactory. This has contributed to eroding citizens' trust in government and increasing tax non-compliance.

Thus, taxation efforts should go hand in hand with improved service delivery and infrastructure, transparent management of public expenditures, the eradication of inefficient government spending, and enhanced accountability. Notably, the prudent governance of funds can foster citizen trust, engagement, and accountability.

References

Abille, A. B. and Mumuni, S. (2023) 'Tax incentives, ease of doing business and inflows of FDI in Africa: Does governance matter?', *Cogent Economics & Finance*, 11(1), 2164555. Available at: https://doi.org/10.1080/23322039.2022.2164555

Ackers, B. and Adebayo, A. (2022) 'Governance of African state-owned enterprises (SOEs) – Towards Agenda 2063', *Accounting Profession Journal (APAJI)* 4(2), pp. 125-45. Available at: https://ojsapaji.org/index.php/apaji/article/view/46

Ademola, O. J., Dada, S. O. and Akintoye, I. R. (2019) 'Bridging tax gap in Nigeria through taxing high net worth individuals: A myth or reality?' *Journal of Taxation and Economic Development,* 18(3), pp. 1-11.

Agence de Presse Sénégalaise (APS) (2016) 'A cause d'exonérations fiscales et douanières accordées au secteur minier, Le Sénégal a perdu en 8 ans plus de 400 milliards de francs CFA, selon les autorités', *Centre de Ressources sur les Entreprises et les Droits de l'Homme*, 6 décembre. Available at: https://www.business-humanrights.org/fr

Agence Nationale de la Statistique et de la Démographie (ANSD) (2014) *Rapport definitif : Recensement général de la population et de l'habitat, de l'agriculture et de l'elevage (RGPHAE) 2013*. Available at: https://ireda.ceped.org/inventaire/ressources/sen-2013-rec-o1_rapport-definitif.pdf

Agyeman, N. K. (2022) 'State loses GH₵27bn to tax exemptions - Finance Minister confirms in parliament', *Graphic Online*, 19 July. Available at: https://www.graphic.com.gh/news/general-news/state-loses-gh-27bn-to-tax-exemptions-finance-minister-confirms-in-parliament.html.

Ali-Nakyea, A. and Amoh, J. (2018) 'Have the generous tax incentives in the natural resource sector been commensurate with FDI flows? A critical analysis from an emerging economy', *International Journal of Critical Accounting*, 10(3/4), pp. 257-273.

Andoh, F. K. (2017) 'Taxable capacity and effort of Ghana's value-added tax', *African Review of Economics and Finance,* 9(2), pp. 255-284.

Andoh, F. K. and Nkrumah, R. K. (2022) 'Distributional aspects of Ghana's value-added tax', *Forum for Social Economics,* 51(4), pp. 394-414. Available at: https://doi.org/10.1080/07360932.2021.1977970

Andoh, S. K. *et al.* (2019) 'Performance of state-owned enterprises: A comparative analysis of Ethiopian Airlines and Ghana Airways', *American Journal of Management*, 19(5), pp. 141-156.

Appiah-Kubi, K. (2001) 'State-owned enterprises and privatisation in Ghana', *The Journal of Modern African Studies*, 39(2), pp. 197-229.

Asiedu, J. (2022) 'Ghana parliament passes tax exemptions bill, 2022', *Ghana Financial Market*, 26 July. Available at: https://ghanafinancialmarket.wordpress.com/2022/07/26/ghana-parliament-passes-tax-exemptions-bill-2022/

Assibey-Mensah, G. O. (1999) 'The value-added tax in Ghana', *Public Budgeting & Finance,* 19(2), pp. 76-89. Available at: https://doi.org/10.1046/j.0275-1100.1999.01164.x

African Tax Administration Forum (ATAF) (2021) *2021 African tax outlook (ATO) publication: Building resilience to global shocks across tax administration.* Pretoria, South Africa: African Tax Administration Forum (ATAF). Available at: https://events.ataftax.org/includes/preview.php?file_id=155&language=en_US

Ba, M. (2023) 'Senelec : un chiffre d'affaires en hausse de 886 milliards FCFA', *Pulse Senegal*, 4 août. Available at: https://www.pulse.sn/business/senelec-un-chiffre-daffaires-en-hausse-de-886-milliards-fcfa/ytckqds

Baafi, A. A. (2022) 'Govt urged to invest more to build strong tax infrastructure', *Graphic*, 12 July. Available at: https://www.graphic.com.gh/business/business-news/govt-urged-to-invest-more-to-build-strong-tax-infrastructure.html

Barma, A. Y. (2019) 'Cameroun : le gouvernement s'attaque à la réduction des dépenses fiscales', *La Tribune Afrique*, 14 août. Available at: https://afrique.latribune.fr/economie/budget-fiscalite/2019-08-14/cameroun-le-gouvernement-s-attaque-a-la-reduction-des-depenses-fiscales-825796.html

BBC News Afrique (2017) 'Sénégal : vers une baisse du prix de l'électricité', 1 janvier. Available at: https://www.bbc.com/afrique/region-38484861

Blunt, M. E. (1970) 'State enterprise in Nigeria and Ghana: The end of an era?' *African Affairs*, 69(274), pp. 27-43.

Cameroun Actuel (2023) 'Dépenses fiscales : 439 milliards de FCFA concédés aux entreprises et ménages', 14 mars. Available at: https://camerounactuel.com/depenses-fiscales-439-milliards-de-fcfa-concedes-aux-entreprises-et-menages/

Cheeseman, N. and Burbidge, D. (2016) 'Are leaders or legislation the silver bullet for counties to succeed?', *Daily Nation*, 1 October Available at: http://www.nation.co.ke/oped/Opinion/are-leaders-or-legislation-silver-bullet-for-counties-to-succeed/440808-3402006-fmthhwz/index.html.

Cheeseman, N. and Griffiths, R. (2005) *Increasing tax revenue in sub-Saharan Africa: The case of Kenya*. OCGG economy analysis No. 06. Oxford, UK: The Oxford Council of Good Governance.

Collier, P. *et al.* (2018) *Land and property taxes for municipal finance*. IGC working paper. London: International Growth Centre. Available at: https://www.theigc.org/wp-content/uploads/2017/08/Land-and-Property-Taxes-for-Municipal-Finance-06.07.18.pdf

Coulibaly, S. and Camara, A. (2021) *Taxation, foreign direct investment and spillover effects in the mining sector*. Working paper No. 354. Abidjan, Côte d'Ivoire: African Development Bank Group.

Decoster, A. *et al.* (2010) 'How regressive are indirect taxes? A microsimulation analysis for five European countries', *Journal of Policy Analysis and Management*, 29(2), pp. 326-350.

Di John, J. (2006) *The political economy of taxation and tax reform in developing countries*. UNU-WIDER research paper. Available at: https://www.econstor.eu/handle/10419/63561

Diallo, F. Z. (2023) 'Après des pertes mensuelles de 6 à 7 milliards en 2022 : Air Sénégal sort la tête de l'eau', *EnQuete+*, 18 juillet. Available at: https://www.enqueteplus.com/content/apr%C3%A8s-des-pertes-mensuelles-de-6-%C3%A0-7-milliards-en-2022-air-s%C3%A9n%C3%A9gal-sort-la-t%C3%AAte-de-l%E2%80%99eau

Dietz, C. (2023) 'Number of African millionaires to rise 42% over next decade, says report', *African Business*, 20 April. Available at: https://african.business/2023/04/quick-reads/number-of-african-millionaires-to-rise-by-42-by-2032-says-report

Direction Générale des Impôts (DGI) (2022) 'Mobilisation des recettes fiscales au 30 novembre 2022 : La trés bonne performance de La DGI,' *DGI News*, 4 décembre.

Direction Générale des Impôts et des Domaines (DGID) (2020) 'Programme Yaatal. Yaatal Natt, Teggi Yokkuté' Direction Générale des Impôts et Domaines.

Djotié, J. R. (2022) 'Réformes fiscales : Le plan triennal de modernisation du système fiscal camerounais validé', *Eco-Finances*, 29 décembre. Available at: https://ecofinances.net/2022/12/29/reformes-fiscales-le-plan-triennal-de-modernisation-du-systeme-fiscal-camerounais-valide/

Effah, E. (2021) 'Landlords to start paying taxes on rent soon - GRA', *Pulse Ghana*, 14 June. Available at: https://www.pulse.com.gh/business/gra-to-introduce-rent-tax-soon/klpwcs4

Fjeldstad, O.-H., Ali, M. and Goodfellow, T. (2017) *Taxing the urban boom: Property taxation in Africa*. Bergen, Norway: Chr. Michelsen Institute. Available at: https://open.cmi.no/cmi-xmlui/handle/11250/2475392

Francis, T. (2021) 'The poor and venerable suffers the most: 57% of tax revenue comes from indirect taxes over the past 10 years', *The Business & Financial Times*, 10 November. Available at: https://thebftonline.com/2021/11/10/the-poor-and-venerable-suffers-the-most-57-of-tax-revenue-comes-from-indirect-taxes-over-the-past-10-years/

Franzsen, R. and McCluskey, W. (2017) *Property tax in Africa: Status, challenges, and prospects*. Washington, DC: Lincoln Institute of Land Policy.

Fualdes, N. (2023) 'Moins d'Europe, plus d'Amérique : le nouveau cap d'Air Sénégal,' *jeuneafrique*, 19 juillet. Available at: https://www.jeuneafrique.com/1464826/economie-entreprises/moins-deurope-plus -damerique-le-nouveau-cap-dair-senegal/

Ghana Revenue Authority (GRA) (n.d.) *VAT standard*. Available at: https://gra.gov.gh/domestic-tax/tax-types/ vat-standard/

Global Tax Expenditure Database (GTED) (2021) *Ghana*. Available at: https://gted.net/country-profile/ghana/

Gouvernement du Sénégal (2014) *Plan Sénégal Émergent*. Available at: https://www.finances.gouv.sn/ publication/plan-senegal-emergent-pse/

Harcourt, S. (2024) 'Official development assistance (ODA)', *ONE Data & Analysis*, 29 September. Available at: https://data.one.org/topics/official-development-assistance/

Iddrisu, A. M. *et al.* (2021) *A survey of the Ghanaian tax system*. Accra: Institute of Fiscal Studies and Ministry of Finance, Ghana. Available at: https://mofep.gov.gh/news-and-events/2021-03-11/survey-of-the -ghanaian-tax-system

Jacquemot, P. and Raffinot, M. (2018) 'La mobilisation fiscale en Afrique', *Revue d'économie financière,* 131(3), pp. 243-263. Available at: https://doi.org/10.3917/ecofi.131.0243

Jibao, S. and Prichard, W. (2013) *Rebuilding local government finance after conflict: The political economy of property tax reform in post-conflict Sierra Leone*. International Centre for Tax and Development working paper No. 12. Sussex, UK: International Centre for Tax and Development.

Kamer, L. (n.d.) 'Africa: Number of millionaires by country 2022', *Statista*. Available at: https://www.statista. com/statistics/1182842/number-of-high-net-worth-individuals-in-africa-by-country/

Kangave, J. *et al.* (2016) *Boosting revenue collection through taxing high net worth individuals: The case of Uganda*. ICTD Working paper No. 45. Brighton, UK: Institute of Development Studies. Available at: https://papers. ssrn.com/sol3/papers.cfm?abstract_id=2776590

Knebelmann, J. (2019) *Taxing property owners in Dakar*. Policy brief No. 50415. London, UK: International Growth Centre. Available at: https://www.theigc.org/wp-content/uploads/2019/11/50415-policy-brief -2019.pdf

Ministère des Finances du Cameroun (MINFI) (2020) *La Taxe sur la Valeur Ajoutée (TVA) en bref*. Available at: https://minfi.gov.cm/la-taxe-sur-la-valeur-ajoutee-tva-en-bref/

Ministère des Finances (2019) *Rapport sur les dépenses fiscales de l'exercice 2019*. Cameroon: Ministère des Finances du Cameroun.

Ministère des Finances et du Budget (2020) *Rapport d'évaluation sur les dépenses fiscales*. Dakar, Sénégal: Ministère des Finances et du Budget du Sénégal.

Ministry of Finance (n.d.) *2020 State ownership report*. Accra: Ministry of Finance. Available at: https://mofep. gov.gh/sites/default/files/news/2020_State_Ownership_Report.pdf

Moe, T. M. (2005) 'Power and political institutions', *Perspectives on Politics* 3(2), pp. 215-233. Available at: http://ereserve.library.utah.edu/Annual/POLS/6003/Francis/power.pdf

Mbodiam, B. R. (2022) 'Impôts : les recettes non pétrolières franchissent les 2 000 milliards de FCFA pour la première fois au Cameroun', *Investir au Cameroun*, 23 décembre. Available at: https://www. investiraucameroun.com/economie/2312-18884-impots-les-recettes-non-petrolieres-franchissent -les-2-000 -milliards-de-fcfa-pour-la-premiere-fois-au-cameroun

Moore, M. (2015) *Tax and the governance dividend*. ICTD Working paper No. 37. Sussex, UK: Institute of Development Studies. Available at: https://papers.ssrn.com/abstract=2634034

Moore, M., Prichard, W. and Fjeldstad, O.-H. (2018a) *Taxing Africa: Coercion, reform and development*. 1st edn. New York: Bloomsbury Publishing. Available at: https://www.bloomsbury.com/ca/taxing-africa -9781783604548/

Moore, M., Prichard, W. and Fjeldstad, O.-H. (2018b) *Taxing Africa. Coercion, reform and development*. Chicago: The University of Chicago Press. Available at: https://press.uchicago.edu/ucp/books/book/distributed/T/ bo28633229.html

Mutize, M. and Tefera, E. (2020) 'The governance of state-owned enterprises in Africa: An analysis of selected cases', *Journal of Economics and Behavioral Studies*, 12(2), pp. 9-16.

Nga Nga, F. and Ebele Ombede, E. T. (2022) 'The governance of Cameroonian public enterprises under the scanner: A reading on the effectiveness of performance contracts', *Revue Du Contrôle, de La Comptabilité et de l'audit*, 6(4), pp. 328-349.

Nyarko Otoo, K. (2020) *Tackling tax incentives, Ghana*. Casablanca, Morocco: Public Services International. Available at: https://publicservices.international/resources/publications/tackling-tax-incentives -ghana?id=10560&lang=en

Nyirakamana, C. (2021) *Incentives, rules, power, and discretion: A comparative analysis of local financial autonomy building in the cities of Accra and Nairobi*. Unpublished PhD thesis. McMaster University. Available at: https://macsphere.mcmaster.ca/handle/11375/26337

Organisation de coopération et de développement économiques (OCDE) (2017) 'Vers une administration publique opérant comme catalyseur du développement social et économique sénégalais', in *Examen multidimensionnel du Sénégal. Volume 2. Analyse approfondie et recommandations*. Paris : Éditions OECD, pp. 125-147. Available at: https://doi.org/10.1787/9789264287082-9-fr

OECD (2018) *Tax policies for inclusive growth: Prescription versus practice*. OECD Economic Policy Paper. Available at: https://www.oecd.org/content/dam/oecd/en/publications/reports/2018/12/tax-policies-for-inclusive-growth_4df639c9/09ba747a-en.pdf

OECD (2019) 'Senegal/Sénégal', in *Revenue statistics in Africa 2019*. Paris: OECD Publishing, pp. 227-228. Available at: https://www-oecd-ilibrary-org.ezp.lib.cam.ac.uk/taxation/data/oecd-tax-statistics/revenue-statistics-in-africa-senegal-edition-2019_30f5f287-en.

OECD, African Union Commission (AUC) and African Tax Administration Forum (ATAF) (2022) *Revenue statistics in Africa 2022*. Paris: OECD Publications. Available at: https://www.oecd.org/en/publications/revenue-statistics-in-africa-2022_ea66fbde-en-fr.html

OECD, ATAF and CUA (2022) 'Cameroun', in *Statistiques des recettes publiques en Afrique 2022*. Paris : Éditions OECD. Available at: https://www.oecd.org/fr/publications/revenue-statistics-in-africa-2022_ea66fbde-en-fr.html

Olugbade, O. A. *et al.* (2021) *State-owned enterprises in Middle East, North Africa, and Central Asia: Size, costs, and challenges*. Departmental Papers No. 019. Washington, DC: IMF. Available at: https://www.elibrary.imf.org/view/journals/087/2021/019/article-A001-en.xml

Prichard, W. (2019) 'Tax, politics, and the social contract in Africa', *Oxford research encyclopedia of politics*. Available at: https://doi.org/10.1093/acrefore/9780190228637.013.853

Prichard, W., Kamara, A. B. and Meriggi, N. (2020) 'Freetown just implemented a new property tax system that could quintuple revenue, *International Centre for Tax and Development (ICTD)*, 22 May. Available at: https://www.ictd.ac/blog/freetown-new-property-tax-system-quintuple-revenue/

Publish What you Pay (PWYP) (2018) 'Cameroon is losing millions a year due to tax exemptions', 23 May. Available at: https://www.pwyp.org/pwyp-news/cameroon-tax-exemptions/

Qhobosheane, L. A-M. (2018) *The impact of political interference in state-owned companies: A case study on SABC*. Unpublished master's thesis. University of the Free State. Available at: https://scholar.ufs.ac.za/server/api/core/bitstreams/adb14807-710c-4a0c-a785-f88d29ba6d85/content

Republic of Ghana (2019) *Ghana beyond aid charter and strategy document*. Accra: The Republic of Ghana.

Republic of Ghana (2021) *The budget statement and economic policy of the Government of Ghana for the 2021 financial year*. Accra: Ministry of Finance. Available at: https://mofep.gov.gh/budget-statements/2021

République du Cameroun (n.d.) *Rapport d'exécution du budget de l'état pour l'exercice 2020*. Cameroun : Ministère des Finances du Cameroun. Available at: https://www.minfi.gov.cm/wp-content/uploads/2021/08/RAPPORT_EXECUTION_Budget_2020.pdf

République du Sénégal (2018) *Plan Sénégal Émergent : Plans d'actions prioritaires 2019-2023*. Dakar, Sénégal : Ministère de l'Économie, des Finances et du Plan.

République du Sénégal (2021) *Rapport trimestriel d'exécution budgetaire : Quatrième trimestre 2020*. Dakar, Sénégal : Ministère des Finances et du Budget du Sénégal.

Rogan, M. *et al.* (2023) 'Ghana's e-levy is unfair to the poor and misses its revenue target: A lesson in mobile money tax design', *The Conversation*, 27 March. Available at: http://theconversation.com/ghanas-e-levy-is-unfair-to-the-poor-and-misses-its-revenue-target-a-lesson-in-mobile-money-tax-design-201303.

Santoro, F., Abounabhan, M. , and Diouf, A. (2022) 'Ghana's new e-levy: The sour, sweet and switches so far', *ICTD*, 4 August. Available at: https://www.ictd.ac/blog/ghana-e-levy-sour-sweet-switches/

Segbefia, S. (2021) 'GRA taps data scientists to go after tax deviants... especially high-net-worth individuals', *The Business & Financial Times*, 26 January. Available at: https://thebftonline.com/2021/01/26/gra-taps-data-scientists-to-go-after-tax-deviants-especially-high-net-worth-individuals/

Segura-Ubiergo, A. *et al.* (2018) 'Domestic revenue mobilization in Africa: What are the possibilities?' in *Regional economic outlook: Sub-Saharan Africa: Domestic revenue mobilization and private investment.* Washington, DC: IMF, pp. 31-58. Available at: https://www.imf.org/en/Publications/REO/SSA/Issues/2018/04/30/sreo0518

Slack, E. and Bird, R. M. (2014) *The political economy of property tax reform.* OECD working papers on fiscal federalism. Available at: https://www.oecd-ilibrary.org/taxation/the-political-economy-of-property-tax-reform_5jz5pzvzv6r7-en

Slemrod, J. (1990) 'Optimal taxation and optimal tax systems', *Journal of Economic Perspectives,* 4(1), pp. 157-78. Available at: https://doi.org/10.1257/jep.4.1.157

Suits, D. B. (1977) 'Measurement of tax progressivity', *The American Economic Review,* 67(4), pp. 747-752.

Tanzi, V. *et al.* (1981) 'Special tax incentives', in *Taxation in Sub-Saharan Africa.* Washington, DC: International Monetary Fund, pp. 33-36. Available at: https://www.elibrary.imf.org/display/book/9781557750815/ch007.xml

Tefera, M. G. and Odhiambo, N. M. (2022) 'The impact of foreign aid on economic growth in Africa: Empirical evidence from low income countries', *Forum for Development Studies,* 49(2), pp. 175-210. Available at: https://doi.org/10.1080/08039410.2022.2080760

Trading Economics (n.d.) *Cameroon corporate tax rate - 2022 data - 2023 forecast - 2004-2021 historical - chart.* Available at: https://tradingeconomics.com/cameroon/corporate-tax-rate

United Nations Conference on Trade and Development (UNCTAD) (2024) 'Development aid hits record high but falls in developing countries', 11 April. Available at: https://www.unctad.org/news/development-aid-hits-record-high-falls-developing-countries.

Zeng, D. Z. (2015) *Global experiences with special economic zones: Focus on China and Africa.* Policy Research Working Papers. Washington, DC: World Bank. Available at: https://doi.org/10.1596/1813-9450-7240

CHAPTER 4

From Tax Competition to Cooperation?

4.1. Introduction

African countries have experienced a sudden slowdown in their economies due to the Covid-19 pandemic and successive crises. This has further exacerbated Africa's low levels of domestic resource mobilization (DRM) and has hindered the continent's efforts to mobilize resources. Covid-19 has negatively impacted Africa in key sectors such as tourism, education, manufacturing, accommodation, and food services, construction, mining, arts, and entertainment. This has resulted in the decline of tax revenues, foreign direct investments (FDI), remittances and aid flows, and increased the risk of debt unsustainability and default in Africa. In addition to the Covid-19 pandemic African countries had already been facing key challenges in mobilizing and retaining resources which included shrinking tax bases;[68] relying on few tax heads or overreliance on extractive/commodity taxes; ineffective tax systems; inadequate tax administrative capacity; outdated tax policies; tax expenditure eroding tax bases; and illicit financial flows (IFFs) out of Africa.

Furthermore, African economies have long faced the challenge of attracting investment from multinational corporations (MNCs) to stimulate growth and provide jobs while raising taxes from the returns on such investment given their huge financing needs.

The continent needs to tap into its own wealth to finance the African Union's Agenda 2063 which aims at ensuring positive socio-economic transformation within the next 40 years. In this agenda, Africa's responsibility for its own development is under the spotlight. Funding Agenda 2063 requires a combination of strategies and efforts from African governments, private sector entities, and

---

68 Africa's tax base erosion is driven by internal policy failures and external factors. Internally, governments weaken their tax base through poor tax incentives, non-transparent contracts in extractive industries, inadequate taxation of high-net-worth individuals, and reliance on single-source taxation. Lack of automated tax systems and the disconnect between tax policy and administration further exacerbate the issue. Externally, trade misinvoicing, involving fraudulent invoicing of trade transactions, accounts for significant illicit financial flows, draining crucial domestic resources needed for development. The large informal sector and lack of inter-regional cooperation in information exchange also contribute to tax base erosion (ATAF (2014): *Cross-Border Taxation: Implications for Africa: African Priorities on Base Erosion and Profit Shifting*).

international partners. One of these strategies is to prioritize domestic resource mobilization by increasing tax revenues and reducing illicit financial flows.

International tax cooperation is considered a key prerequisite for domestic mobilization of resources in developed and developing countries alike, as governments worldwide are faced with the consequences of economic globalization. In addition, international tax governance is necessary to ensure consistent adoption, interpretation and implementation of international standards required to tackle the global effect of IFFs and build tax certainty to foster economic growth. It is an issue that can only be addressed through a collective response from governments, with no single country able to address it on a stand-alone basis, as unilateral approaches may have damaging effects on trade and the economy.

The global tax deal reached under the auspices of the Inclusive Framework for BEPS Implementation (IF) in October 2021 is perhaps the most significant global tax reform in a century that sought to introduce a new international tax regime that would ensure taxes are paid where economic activity takes place rather than the physical location or residence. The Inclusive Framework was created with the objectives of leveling the playing field for all committed (interested) and relevant jurisdictions and ensure that they are involved on an equal footing in the setting of future standards relating to BEPS issues, implementing and monitoring of the BEPS outcomes, including tailoring implementation solutions for BEPS outcomes that are appropriate for all capacity levels.

More recently, new proposals for strengthening international tax cooperation in a more inclusive and effective way following the adoption of the resolution on Promotion of Inclusive and Effective Tax Cooperation at the United Nations (A/RES/77/244) have emerged.

Box 5. Fiscal challenges and opportunities in African economies amid global uncertainty

In a complex global economic system, taxing activities has become difficult and costly, weakening the ability of many countries to provide public services or redistribute wealth (Poitevin, 2018; Commission européenne, 2001). The global economic downturn and the pandemic crisis increased fiscal uncertainty in Africa, which has experienced declines in tax rates and revenues since 1980 (Keen and Brumby, 2017). Factors such as unsuitable fiscal systems, lack of trust in institutions, and the negative relationship between natural resources and tax revenues contribute to low fiscal revenue mobilization (Niang, 2020; Belinga, Melou and Nganou, 2017; Ajayi and Ndikumana, 2015). In addition, fiscal competition poses a real threat to public revenues and the budgetary balance of developing countries. There is an urgent need to mobilize internal resources for development, with a World Bank estimate of US$93 billion per year required for infrastructure in Africa. The Covid-19 crisis calls for sub-regional integration and cooperation (ECOWAS, CEMAC, SADC, AfCFTA, etc.) to strengthen economic resilience and achieve development goals.

Chapter 4 explores ways to reduce tax competition through better cooperation between African countries and globally and the potential contribution of global tax initiatives to fighting tax evasion and increasing resource mobilization, particularly in the extractive industry. It begins by outlining the importance of tax revenues for African countries and then proceeds to highlight the importance of corporate taxes for their economies, a substantial part of which is paid by multinational corporations. The next section of the chapter explores the impacts of tax competition in Africa, highlighting short-term benefits versus long-term negative impacts on government revenue and regional disparities. Subsequent sections of the chapter seek to review the advantages and limitations of the international tax rules offered by the Inclusive Framework initiative for African countries as well as the opportunities and risks posed by the promotion of inclusive and effective tax cooperation at the UN. They examine the current debate on international tax rules and some regional initiatives with a view to providing recommendations on what countries in the continent could do.

4.2. Importance of tax revenues for African countries

Taxation has been the conventional way for governments all over the world to raise revenues in order to fund countries' development agendas and pay for the delivery of public services including education, healthcare, regulation, social protection and security. Tax revenues are also used to build public infrastructure such as roads, bridges, schools, hospitals, power projects, broadband, etc. Governments also use the resources available to them for public investment including in state owned enterprises and pension schemes.

In addition to revenues, governments also use tax to influence behavior. They accordingly levy sin taxes on things like cigarettes, alcohol and environmental pollution and subsidize things like investment, education, and pensions. Tax also has an inextricable link to governance in the sense that in strong tax systems, governments strive to be accountable for the use of taxpayer funds while taxpayers themselves pay close attention to the workings of government. A fair and effective tax system is necessary for building trust between citizens and their governments, which is a crucial element of the fiscal social contract and necessary for the development of democratic institutions (Monkam, 2011). Furthermore, when governments are able to raise taxes to meet their obligations the amount that they have to borrow is reduced.

The composition of tax revenues varies widely across countries and regions in Africa, depending on factors such as the structure of the economy, the tax system in place, and the level of informal economic activity. In general, African countries tend to rely heavily on indirect taxes such as value-added taxes (VAT) and customs duties, rather than direct taxes such as income taxes (Figure 24). This is because consumption taxes are easier to collect and administer and can generate significant revenue even in economies with high levels of informality. It is also partly because of low levels of formal employment in many African countries which makes it difficult for governments to collect income taxes from a large portion of the workforce.

Figure 24: Tax structures in Africa in 2020, percent of total tax revenues

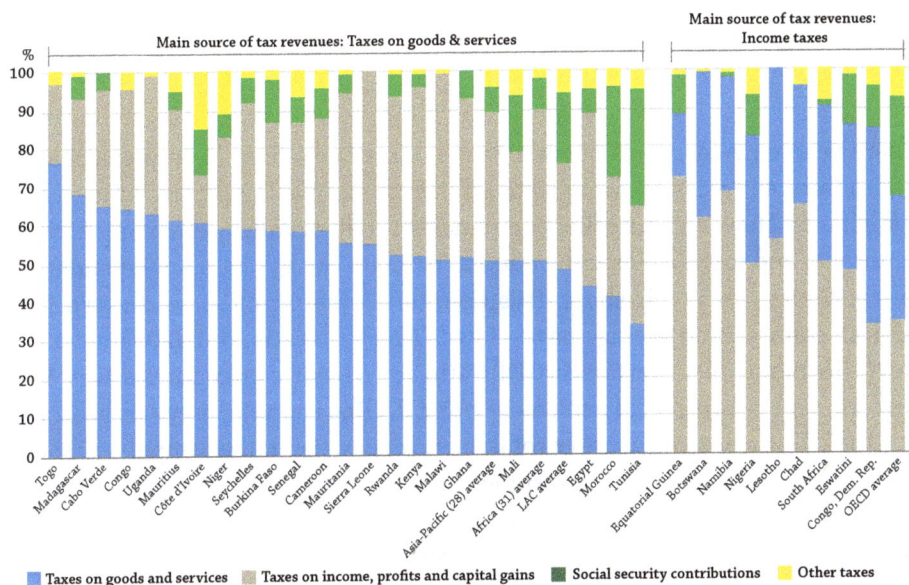

Source: ATAF/AU/OECD Revenue Statistics in Africa (2022)

In many African countries, the tax base is relatively narrow, meaning that there are relatively few individuals and companies that earn enough income to be subject to income taxes. This is partly due to the fact that many African economies are still developing, and that there are relatively few large, formal firms. In 2015, few large taxpayers accounted for very high shares of government revenue in some African countries (Figure 25).

Figure 25: Large taxpayers' share of total government revenue in Africa, 2015

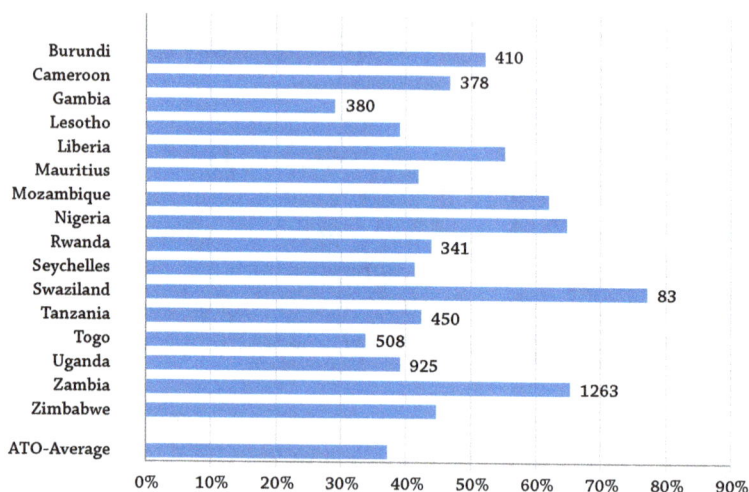

Source: ATAF (2017)

There is some evidence to suggest that tax revenues have been increasing in Africa in recent years, in part due to efforts to improve tax administration and compliance. However, tax collection remains a major challenge in many African countries, and more needs to be done to broaden the tax base and ensure that everyone pays their fair share. It is therefore a matter of some concern that African countries on average have a low tax-to-GDP ratio. In 2020, amidst the Covid-19 pandemic, the tax-to-GDP ratio for 31 African countries was 16.0 percent, representing a 0.3 percentage point decline from the previous year. The tax-to-GDP ratio is a measure of total tax revenues, including compulsory social security contributions, as a percentage of GDP. Compared to Asian and Pacific economies (19.1 percent), Latin America and the Caribbean (21.9 percent), and the OECD (33.5 percent), the Africa (31) average was lower (Figure 26).

There are several reasons for the low tax-to-GDP rate in Africa including notably the size of the informal economy and the weakness of tax administration. The informal sector, which consists of activities that have market value and would contribute to tax revenue and GDP if included in the formal economy, accounts for about 35 percent of GDP in low-income countries as opposed to barely 15 percent in advanced economies.

Figure 26: Tax revenues in Africa, 2020 (percent of GDP)*

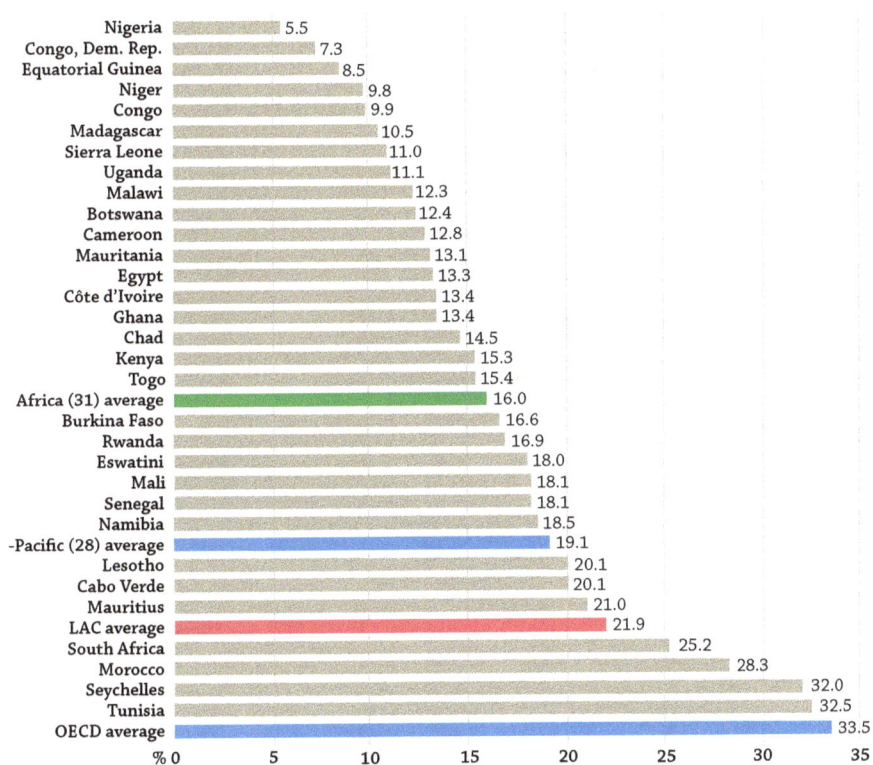

Nigeria	5.5
Congo, Dem. Rep.	7.3
Equatorial Guinea	8.5
Niger	9.8
Congo	9.9
Madagascar	10.5
Sierra Leone	11.0
Uganda	11.1
Malawi	12.3
Botswana	12.4
Cameroon	12.8
Mauritania	13.1
Egypt	13.3
Côte d'Ivoire	13.4
Ghana	13.4
Chad	14.5
Kenya	15.3
Togo	15.4
Africa (31) average	16.0
Burkina Faso	16.6
Rwanda	16.9
Eswatini	18.0
Mali	18.1
Senegal	18.1
Namibia	18.5
-Pacific (28) average	19.1
Lesotho	20.1
Cabo Verde	20.1
Mauritius	21.0
LAC average	21.9
South Africa	25.2
Morocco	28.3
Seychelles	32.0
Tunisia	32.5
OECD average	33.5

Source: ATAF/AU/OECD Revenue Statistics in Africa (2022)
Note: * The Africa (31) average should be interpreted with caution as data for social security contributions are not available or are partial in a few countries (ATAF/AU/OECD, 2022).

4.2.1. Importance of corporate taxes for African countries

One key feature of Africa's low tax-to-GDP ratio is the degree of dependence on corporate income tax (CIT) on the continent (Ocampo, 2018). Whereas receipts from personal income tax in developed economies are over double those from corporate income tax, the same cannot be said for Africa, where corporate income tax brings in more revenues for governments (Table 7).

In general, sources suggest that CIT revenue as a percentage of GDP in Africa is generally lower compared to other regions of the world, indicating that there is significant potential for African countries to improve their tax revenue mobilization efforts. According to the World Bank's World Development Indicators database, the average CIT revenue as a percentage of GDP in Africa was 2.9 percent in 2019. By comparison, the average for high-income countries was

2.8 percent; the average for Latin America and the Caribbean was 3.3 percent; and the average for the Middle East and North Africa was 4.2 percent. When comparing the CIT revenue as a percentage of GDP in Africa in 2019 between resource-rich and non-resource rich economies, it amounted to 4.7 percent and 2.8 percent respectively. This difference is explained, among other factors, by the high profitability of resource industries.

Table 7. Tax structures in Africa vs economies of other regions (2020)

	Tax-to-GDP ratio	Corporate income tax to total revenue	Personal income tax to total revenue	VAT to total revenue
OECD	33.5%	9.6%	23.5%	20.3%
Asia	19.1%	18.8%	16.0%	23.1%
Latin America and Caribbean	21.9%	15.6%	9.8%	27.5%
Africa	16.0%	19.3%	18.5%	27.8%

Source: OECD Revenue Statistics in Asia and the Pacific (2022)

Despite the key contribution of corporate income taxes, there has been a global decline in their levels. For instance, since the 1980s the unweighted global average corporate income tax rate has fallen from about 40 percent to 23.4 percent today. The fall in average corporate tax rates quite naturally affects African countries which are more reliant on them for raising revenues. Also noteworthy is the fact that the biggest corporate actors in African countries are mostly MNCs who contribute about 23 percent of such taxes. A falling tax rate also means that to increase revenues or even keep them constant, the tax net must be widened. This poses an additional dilemma in environments with large informal sectors and inadequate tax administration as well as the tax eroding effects of profit shifting and tax competition, which are driving a race to the bottom.

Several factors may contribute to the decline of the CIT revenue as a percentage of GDP in Africa over time. First, tax incentives implemented to attract foreign investment often reduce the tax base and lower the revenue generated from CIT. Tax incentives are a major contributor to the decline of CIT revenue in Africa and they are often poorly designed, leading to revenue leakage and reduced effect-iveness in attracting investment (UN and CIAT, 2018). Second, large informal economies in many African countries may limit the revenue generated from CIT as many informal businesses operate outside the tax system. Third, MNCs may engage in transfer pricing practices to shift profits to lower tax jurisdictions, reducing the revenue generated from CIT in African countries. For example, in its

2022 report, the Independent Commission for Reform of International Corporate Tax (ICRICT) contended that the international financial system's structural inadequacies have permitted as much as 10 percent of global GDP to be concealed in tax havens, allowing the richest 1 percent (who possess up to 40 percent of the wealth in certain nations) to circumvent as much as 25 percent of their income tax obligations by utilizing offshore arrangements (Ocampo, 2018; ICRICT, 2022). Finally, weak tax administration and enforcement may also contribute to the decline of CIT revenue in Africa. According to the World Bank's 2020 *Doing Business* report, African countries on average have lower tax administration and enforcement scores compared to other regions. This indicates that tax collection and compliance measures tend to be weaker in Africa, which can result in lower tax revenue collection for governments (World Bank, 2020).

Consequently, the way MNCs are taxed is a matter of great importance for African economies. On one hand, countries want to attract these corporations as sources of investment and economic benefits. However, given the size, complexity of operations and superior legal, financial, and accounting capacities of multinational corporations, it is difficult for African countries to track, trace, and monitor their behavior, especially relating to tax. For instance, the annual revenue of Amazon, which was about US\$432 billion in 2021, was comparable to the GDP of Nigeria (US\$440 billion) which is Africa's largest economy.

In conclusion, the African continent is home to several developing nations with limited resources to develop their economies, which makes it critical for them to maximize their tax revenue collection from MNCs. International tax cooperation is therefore essential for better taxation in Africa.

4.3. The tax competition landscape in Africa

4.3.1. Tax competition and incentives in Africa

African nations encounter various difficulties in efficiently taxing diverse business segments within their borders. Taxing the informal sector, small and medium-sized enterprises (SMEs), and MNCs poses distinct challenges. Hence, it is crucial for these countries to establish cohesive, evidence-driven tax policies that strike a balance between generating revenue, ensuring strong governance, and fostering an environment that promotes business and economic expansion. As a result, they engage in tax competition by offering tax incentives and exemptions to attract foreign investment, often at the expense of other countries. This can lead to a race to the bottom, where countries continuously lower their tax rates to remain competitive. Furthermore, the tax base in Africa is often significantly eroded by the granting of inappropriate and wasteful tax incentives.

Box 6. Perspectives on fiscal incentives

While initial studies were skeptical about the influence of fiscal incentives on foreign investment (Gubian, Guillaumat-Taillet and Le Cacheux, 1986; Muet and Avouyi-Dovi, 1987), more recent research acknowledges positive effects in certain circumstances (Poitevin, 2018; Keen and Brumby, 2017; James, 2017; OCDE, 2002). Hines (2004) concluded that a 1 percent reduction in the effective tax rate could increase FDI by about 2 percent. Kransdorff (2010) emphasizes that the manufacturing sector is particularly sensitive to fiscal incentives. Proponents of fiscal incentives argue that they limit inefficient state spending through the reduction of the tax burden (McLure, 1986) and have similar beneficial effects as price competition between companies. In addition, globalization and technological advancements have increased the elasticity of foreign capital to tax variations, allowing small economies to compete with larger ones by attracting FDI (Kransdorff, 2010; Deblock and Rioux, 2008; Bolnick, 2004; Blomström, Kokko and Mucchielli 2003; Altshuler, Grubert and Newlon, 1998).

Exemptions are granted for specific categories of taxpayers, activities or individual companies and projects. When granted to companies, they are often termed "incentives" because they are technically given to attract new investment, especially from overseas. Exemptions in Africa are particularly widespread, and studies have indicated the continent experiences significant revenue loss through the granting of tax incentives. Consequently, they undermine government efforts to raise adequate domestic resources to finance public services and social protection, address inequality and meet the SDGs. It is posited that because of the perceptible lack of transparency in how incentives are granted and managed, tax incentives should be linked to the IFF agenda (Padilla *et al.*, 2020).

Box 7. The paradox of tax exemptions in attracting foreign investment to Africa

The current situation in many African countries is a race towards tax exemptions to attract foreign investors. However, these exemptions appear to be sought often by those who have already decided to invest, raising questions about their actual impact on increasing foreign investments (Jacquemot and Raffinot, 2018). A study conducted by the IMF in 2015 across seven African countries found that 84 percent of investors stated that their investment decisions were not motivated by tax exemptions. Furthermore, Jacquemot and Raffino (2018) note that these exemptions are numerous and often granted under opaque conditions, undermining the credibility of the fiscal system. Additionally, these exemptions become difficult to challenge even when they deviate from local legislative codes and are incompatible with national industrial policies.

If exemptions are granted, for example, to aid a mining company, it is essential to ensure that they are used strategically and aligned with clearly identified public policy objectives with significant collective utility. This requires clear foundations, transparent procedures approved by more than one national institution, and strict timelines. Regular control and transparent evaluation of their impacts within budgetary processes are also necessary (Kransdorff, 2010). While fiscal incentives may be desirable in the short term, consideration should be given to the development of skills, modernization of transport, communication, and energy infrastructures, according to Kransdorff (2010). These elements are identified as the main determinants of foreign capital's attraction.

4.3.2. Challenges posed by tax competition and incentives in Africa

A study published in 2012 by ActionAid International and TJN-Africa highlighted the substantial loss of money in East Africa resulting from tax expenditures offered to lure FDI. For instance, in 2008 Tanzania incurred a loss of as much as US$1.23 billion, equivalent to 6 percent of its GDP, which could have augmented the national budget for education by one-fifth and the health budget by two-fifths. The report also revealed that Kenya suffered an annual loss of US$1.1 billion, which represents more than twice Kenya's entire health budget and amounted to 3.1 percent of its GDP. From 2009 to 2010, Uganda incurred an annual loss of as much as 2 percent of its GDP, equivalent to about US$272 million, which was almost twice Uganda's whole health budget. Lastly, Rwanda lost US$156 million (3.6 percent of GDP) in 2008 and US$234 million (4.7 percent of GDP) in 2009. These revenue losses could have been used to double spending on education. While not all tax expenditures are detrimental, a considerable portion of these revenue losses resulted from tax incentives granted to attract foreign investment, which mostly benefited large corporations and led to harmful tax competition and a race to the bottom in the region (TJN-Africa and ActionAid International, 2012).

A recent study aimed to evaluate the effectiveness and prudence of Kenya's tax expenditures in light of the country's current fiscal situation. The study's primary goal was to provide reliable information to support advocacy efforts for a more equitable, just, and progressive tax system in the country. In Kenya, tax expenditures (TE) refer to the total revenue forgone by the government as a result of preferential tax measures (tax incentives). By using the revenue forgone approach, the study calculated the difference between the actual tax paid (due to the tax expenditure) and the theoretical tax amount, assuming full compliance with the benchmark tax system (BTS). The study found that tax expenditures as a percentage of GDP in Kenya averaged 4 percent between 2015 and 2020. Furthermore, tax expenditures accounted for 20 percent of potential tax revenue (revenue collected plus tax expenditures) on average between 2017 and 2021, suggesting that annual revenue collection would surpass the tax revenue target by Ksh0.33 trillion if tax expenditures had not been granted. The study offered several key recommendations to promote a fairer, more just, and progressive tax expenditure system in Kenya (TJN-Africa, 2022).

In the ECOWAS region, tax incentives presented mixed results in attracting FDI. Tax Justice Network Africa and ActionAid International (2015) reveal that these incentives have caused significant losses in essential tax revenue, with the average annual tax expenditure in Nigeria, Ghana, and Senegal constituting 3.8 percent of GDP. Meanwhile, IMF research indicates losses of up to US$730 million per year in corporate income tax revenues due to profit shifting in the mining sector. Despite these generous tax incentives, the investment climate is found to be more impactful in attracting investment than fiscal incentives. It underscores the compelling evidence that investing in transport and energy infrastructure has a more substantial impact on FDI flows, yet this area remains deficient in ECOWAS countries. ECOWAS can finance infrastructure deficits by harmonizing fiscal incentives across member countries.

In addition, there is general concern for the extractive sector, especially mining in sub-Saharan Africa where there are several race-to-the-bottom investment incentives which are generally granted without proper cost-benefit analysis and where expected benefits have not materialized. For many resource-rich African countries, it is crucial to obtain a fair share of the profits generated from the exploitation of their natural resources, which are often non-renewable. Taxing natural resources is distinct from other forms of taxation as it involves dividing profits from resource exploitation between the country that owns the resource and the company, often a multinational enterprise, that has the capability to extract, refine and sell the resource. Failure to implement an appropriate tax regime could result in a significant loss of revenue for the country.

A 2022 AfDB review of FDI and spillover effects in the mining sector found that CIT rate cuts applied to mining companies do not necessarily attract FDI to gold and silver projects but may stimulate FDI in neighboring countries. In other words, an increase in the host country's gold and silver FDI inflows may stimulate FDI to gold and silver projects in neighboring countries (Coulibaly and Camara,

2021). Ali-Nakyea and Amoh (2018) concluded that tax incentives in Ghana's natural resource sector have not had their desired impact on FDI flows.

Box 8. Mining taxation and impact in Guinea

The profits from the exploitation of raw materials sometimes reduce the incentive to collect certain mining taxes, especially when the financial rents and other expected returns (including jobs) from these exploitations are substantial. This explains, among others, the multiple, diverse, and extended tax breaks granted by some countries to mining investors. In Guinea, for example, many mining agreements distort mining codes and other legal frameworks regulating the exercise of mining functions. The discretionary measures they contain have often no rational justification, except from a mining point of view; meanwhile, between the volumes of mined products exploited and exported and the corresponding spin-offs, the population is frustrated in terms of revenue. Several generations of Guineans thus find themselves deprived of their rights, to which are added the consequences of the climate degradation related to these mining operations.

Furthermore, Guinea has not yet adhered to major international conventions that could protect the country against predatory behaviors by multinational companies. According to Kransdorff (2010), while fiscal incentives can be crucial in attracting FDI, they pose significant risks to the budgetary revenues of jurisdictions that use them. Guinea's weak mining and fiscal administrations expose the country to substantial risks of abuse and tax evasion strategies. This is evidenced by the disproportionate increase in mining exports over the past decade compared to the financial resources returning to Guinea.

Guinea would benefit from joining global forums on transparency and information exchange for tax purposes to compensate for its administrative capacity gap and access reliable information on the global raw materials market (Zee, Stotsky and Ley, 2002). Deblock and Rioux (2008) identify three harmful effects of fiscal competition: (1) limiting the welfare state and reducing its fiscal capacities, (2) distorting trade and investment, and (3) tax evasion and erosion of the tax base. Joining the fiscal intelligence community can provide important governance tools to protect the tax base, prevent costly economic distortions, and minimize corruption (Flatters, 2005; Bolnick, 2004).

In summary, while fiscal incentives can attract FDI, their improper application could have detrimental effects on the economy of the country employing them.

Furthermore, tax competition can lead to a concentration of investment in certain countries or regions, exacerbating regional disparities and reducing the potential benefits of foreign investment. This can result in a lack of investment in other areas of the country or region, hindering overall economic growth and development. Tax competition can also lead to a lack of transparency and accountability in tax systems, as governments may be more willing to offer favorable treatment to corporations and investors in exchange for investment. This can lead to a perception of corruption and further undermine public trust in government institutions.

Tax experts have been arguing for decades that governments could solve their revenue problems by severely cutting back on tax exemptions. It is likely that many governments, especially in low-income countries, could attract more private investment by granting fewer tax incentives and using the additional revenue to address the key constraints investors and companies face in doing business in their jurisdictions such as inadequate transport and logistics infrastructure, macroeconomic instability, poor institutions (judiciary, free press, civil service), weak governance and markets, poor rule of law, and enforcement of contracts, lack of consistency in the tax regime, lack of transparency in public finances procurement, unskilled workforce, etc. (IDS, 2014).

Overall, Africa's tax competition landscape suggests that while there may be some benefits, such as increased foreign investment, these benefits are often short-term and do not outweigh the negative impacts on government revenue and regional disparities. Therefore, there is a need for greater coordination and cooperation between African countries to prevent a race to the bottom in terms of tax regimes and ensure that foreign investment benefits all regions of the continent.

4.3.3. Rwanda's approach to countering tax competition challenges

To effectively tackle the issue of tax competition among nations, it is imperative for individual countries or regional blocs to craft a well-defined framework aimed at attracting FDI. This framework should be rooted in transparency, serving as a protective measure against the harmful 'race to the bottom' phenomenon that threatens to deplete tax revenues. Achieving such a transparent system requires strong inter-country collaboration. This collaborative effort can take multiple forms, from information-sharing protocols to the establishment of minimum tax rates or the introduction of a standardized code of conduct for taxation.

In addition, countries can alleviate the pressures of tax competition by refining their existing tax systems, especially when these systems themselves present barriers that force countries to resort to tax incentives as a compensatory measure. Rwanda serves as a case in point: it has elevated its business environment—currently ranking as the second most favorable country for doing business in Africa and among the top 50 globally—to include a reformed, simplified, and modernized tax system. Such reforms have significantly bolstered Rwanda's attractiveness to potential investors.

4.3.3.1. Investor-friendly policies

Rwanda has taken substantial steps to make itself competitive by enriching its business climate. Streamlined business registration, robust property rights, and enhanced ease of doing business collectively contribute to making Rwanda an attractive investment destination. The Investment Code, a well-thought-out framework, aims to lure high-quality, sustainable investments that contribute to the economy and create jobs. Developed through broad-based consultations involving various stakeholders, the code encompasses both non-tax and tax incentives customized for key sectors. The Ministry of Finance supervises this process through the Tax Policy Committee, ensuring that the incentives are not discretionary but rather transparent, predefined, adopted through a rigorous process, and published.

4.3.3.2. A transparent incentive framework

During negotiations with potential investors, the Investment Code serves as the foundational document. When special incentives are necessary for projects not initially covered by the code, these are submitted for cabinet approval, ensuring transparency and rigor in the decision-making process. Rwanda is also expanding its network of Double Taxation Avoidance Agreements, particularly with East African Community (EAC) countries, to prevent tax evasion and promote fair competition.

4.3.3.3. Monitoring and evaluation mechanisms

The Ministry of Finance annually publishes a Tax Expenditure Report. This report provides an in-depth analysis of taxes forgone due to various incentives, such as VAT exemptions and preferential tax rates. It also includes a cost-benefit analysis aimed at evaluating the effectiveness of these incentives. Any shortcomings trigger policy revisions to ensure alignment with broader economic goals. Therefore, the Tax Expenditure Report not only sheds light on the financial implications of these incentives but also serves as a catalyst for evidence-based policy adjustments, ultimately contributing to a more efficient and effective tax system.

Rwanda's tax incentive strategy is rooted in five core objectives:

- Enhancing the affordability of essential goods and services (such as health-care, education and agriculture).
- Addressing administrative challenges in tax application (such as defining the value added in financial services or gambling).
- Promoting regional integration and harmonization (such as EAC-wide import duty exemptions).
- Fostering the development and competitiveness of priority sectors (such as transport).
- Generating broader economic benefits, such as job creation, economic growth, knowledge transfer and local production.

4.3.3.4. *Upholding a fair and competitive tax system*

To avoid the temptation of relying solely on tax incentives as the primary factor rendering a country competitive and attractive to investors, it is imperative to establish a tax environment that is characterized by simplicity, fairness, modernization, and transparency. Rwanda's government has been steadfast in its commitment to enhancing both the tax administration and the legal framework, with the overarching goal of aligning the country's tax system and policies with principles of fair taxation and responsible fiscal management.

Rwanda's commitment to a fair and competitive tax system is demonstrated through continuous updates to its tax policies, aligned with business reforms to stimulate investment. For instance:

- Tax policies were revised in tandem with business reforms to effectively promote investments in Rwanda. The Rwandan government has progress-ively reduced its corporate tax rate, making it one of the lowest in the region. This reduction is aimed at encouraging FDI and stimulating economic activ-ity. In 2023, the CIT rate was reduced to 28 percent (from 30 percent), and the target is to reduce it further and scrap most of the tax incentives. In this case, the income tax rate will cease to be a favorable tax treatment granted to specific investors/activities but to all activities.
- Strengthening tax administration: Rwanda has invested in simplifying and modernizing its tax system and tax administration and this is key for compet-ition and improving the business climate.

4.3.3.5. *International cooperation and compliance*

Rwanda is increasingly compliant with global tax standards, including those set by the OECD. It promotes multilateral agreements to facilitate tax information exchange, thus creating a level playing field for businesses. Mandatory tax filing for all businesses, engagement with international initiatives like BEPS, and the implementation of country-by-country reporting (CbcR), transfer pricing rules, and anti-treaty abuse rules are among Rwanda's key strategies to combat tax evasion.

4.4. From tax competition to cooperation?

Apart from the provision of unproductive and unsuitable tax incentives, Africa faces other obstacles in preserving its tax base. These include the inadequate taxation of natural resources and the practice of profit shifting through controlled transactions. To tackle these key challenges and reduce tax competition between African countries, better cooperation and coordination are necessary. Several steps could be taken to create a more level playing field for investment. This would help ensure that companies are not able to avoid their tax obligations and would generate more revenue for governments to invest in social and economic development. For example, African countries should continue working together to harmonize their tax policies particularly with regard to corporate taxation; establish regional tax authorities to oversee tax compliance across borders; enter into joint taxation agreements to avoid double taxation of companies operating in multiple countries; improve information sharing particularly of tax-related information on MNCs; and improve their capacity to enforce tax laws that hold companies accountable for their tax obligations (AUC, 2019; OECD, 2017).

In addition to these steps, establishing a global taxation system that will effectively curb harmful tax competition and tax avoidance by MNCs, especially those that operate digitally is crucial. To enhance the overall efficiency of international tax collaboration, it is essential for the G20/OECD Inclusive Framework (IF) and other global initiatives to give utmost importance to the fundamental challenges that deteriorate the tax bases of developing nations. For their success, genuine and inclusive reform of tax policies and international tax regulations by the global community are imperative (ICRICT, 2020; ATAF, 2021a).

4.4.1. Assessing the fitness of the current international tax regime for Africa

Despite the fact that the United Nations and the Bretton Woods Institutions have been in existence for over 77 years, there is still no universally accepted or widely inclusive platform or organization for global coordination on international taxation issues. This could be attributed to the aftermath of World War II, as the League of Nations, the predecessor body, played a significant role in defining international tax standards that continue to shape the current international tax framework. Between 1923 and 1928, the Financial Committee of the League of Nations produced four reports on double taxation and tax evasion. The 1923 report laid out the principles that were subsequently used to develop international tax treaties, while the other reports served as drafts for the first models of double tax conventions. These principles continue to inform the present international tax system. Since the end of WWII, the process of establishing international tax standards has primarily been spearheaded by the OECD, and more recently, the G20. However, the era of globalization, multinational corporations, international finance, as well as the 2008 financial and economic crisis, has challenged the current global tax framework and revealed its inadequacies.

4.4.1.1. The current international tax regime

The Inclusive Framework, established in 2016 by the OECD and the G20, aims to provide an equal platform for all member countries, including developing nations, to contribute to the development of standards addressing BEPS. BEPS refers to tax planning strategies used by multinational companies to shift profits from high-tax jurisdictions to low-tax jurisdictions, thereby eroding the tax bases of the former. In October 2020, the OECD released a "blueprint" to tackle the tax challenges resulting from the digitalization of the economy through a two-pillar solution:
- Pillar I aims to ensure that multinational corporations pay their fair share of taxes in the countries where they operate, including in African countries. The pillar proposes a new nexus rule that would allocate taxing rights to market jurisdictions where companies have significant economic presence, even if they do not have a physical presence. This can help to increase tax revenues and reduce the incentives for companies to engage in harmful tax practices such as profit shifting.
- Pillar II aims to address the issue of base erosion and profit shifting by multinational corporations, including in African countries. The pillar proposes a global minimum tax (GMT) that would establish a floor for corporate income

tax rates worldwide. This can help to prevent companies from shifting profits to low-tax jurisdictions and eroding tax bases. The pillar also proposes a mechanism for subjecting multinational corporations to additional taxation in countries where they operate if their effective tax rate falls below the GMT (OECD, 2019).

4.4.1.2. Inadequacies of the current international tax regime for Africa

In October 2021, after several years of highly complex and difficult negotiations, the Inclusive Framework (IF) issued its two-pillar solution to address the tax challenges arising from the digitalization of the economy. This agreement represents the most significant changes to the international tax rules in the last 100 years. One hundred and thirty-six countries and jurisdictions (out of the 140 members of the IF), representing more than 90 percent of global GDP, joined the Statement on the Two-Pillar Solution to Address the Tax Challenges Arising from the Digitalization of the Economy. Kenya, Nigeria, Pakistan, and Sri Lanka have not yet joined the agreement.

While the African Tax Administration Forum (ATAF), an international organization of 40 African tax administrations, welcomes this new milestone, the organization expressed concern that Pillar I proposals do not result in a sufficient reallocation of MNC profits to market jurisdictions and called for at least 35 percent of the residual profits to be re-allocated to market jurisdictions. This will redress the current imbalance in the allocation of taxing rights between residence and source jurisdictions, which favors residence jurisdictions to the detriment of source jurisdictions. Regarding Pillar II, the ATAF and the African Union have argued that the minimum global tax rate needs to be at least 20 percent (not the current 15 percent) to reduce artificial profit shifting out of Africa, given that most African countries have a statutory corporate income tax rate between 25 percent and 35 percent. If all the profits of an MNC are taxed at least at 20 percent no matter in which jurisdiction the profits are reported, this will likely reduce opportunities for profit shifting in Africa (ATAF, 2021a; ATAF, 2021b).

4.4.1.3. Other challenges for Africa

While Pillar I and Pillar II of the OECD/G20 Inclusive Framework on BEPS have the potential of contributing significantly to fighting tax evasion and increasing resource mobilization in developed countries, there remain some limitations for African countries that need to be considered in their implementation. To maximize the two-pillar solution's effectiveness, it will be important to address these limitations and to provide adequate support to implement the proposed measures.

- *Implementation challenges*: The implementation of Pillar I and Pillar II may face challenges in African countries due to their complex tax systems and limited administrative capacity. African countries may lack the resources and expertise to effectively implement the proposed measures, which could undermine their effectiveness in addressing tax evasion and increasing resource mobilization (ATAF, 2019).
- *Political resistance*: The proposed measures may face political resistance from some African countries that have traditionally relied on low tax rates to attract foreign investment. These countries may be reluctant to adopt the proposed measures, which could reduce their attractiveness to foreign investors and potentially harm their economic growth.
- *Limited scope*: Pillar I and Pillar II focus primarily on addressing the tax challenges posed by multinational corporations, which may not be the main source of tax evasion and base erosion in some African countries. Domestic tax evasion and corruption may also be significant issues in some African countries, which may require additional measures beyond Pillar I and Pillar II.
- *Limited benefits for some countries*: Pillar I and Pillar II may not provide significant benefits for some African countries that have a small number of multinational corporations operating within their borders. These countries may not have significant taxing rights under Pillar I and may not be subject to the GMT under Pillar II.
- *Pace of change*: Many African countries face a significant challenge due to the rapid pace of change in international tax standards. The implementation of BEPS outcomes requires policy changes that must be approved by Ministries of Finance, which goes beyond mere operational decisions. A concern for countries like these may be widening the gap between the pace of change in global standard setting and their ability to address implementation challenges. This disconnect between standards and reality is making it increasingly challenging for African countries to participate in global processes, to the point where they may refuse to participate despite political agreements being signed (ATAF, 2019).

In addition to the fact that some countries refused to sign the agreement "on the basis that the G20's proposed minimum corporate tax rate of 15 percent is too low", several African and other developing countries are not part of the Inclusive Framework (SAIIA, 2021). Furthermore, "[s]ome tax justice campaigners and other developing countries have rejected the deal, claiming that it too narrowly benefits rich countries while also ignoring the key considerations that were raised by G24 members " (SAIIA, 2021). For example, ICRICT, a global coalition comprising intergovernmental, civil society and labor organizations, has urged for the implementation of a 25 percent global minimum tax rate. According to estimates, this rate would generate an additional US$17 billion annually for the 38 poorest nations, compared to the current 15 percent rate. What is more, several developing countries, despite being signatories to the agreement, have expressed apprehensions regarding the new tax rules, as they are contingent on the removal of any unilateral taxes levied on technology firms. These nations depend heavily on revenue generated from taxes on digital services, which cover a larger number of companies and often generate more revenue than what would be expected under the new system (Mapahatra, 2021).

4.4.1.4. *The current international tax regime and the extractive sector in Africa*

On average, the mining industry has contributed approximately 10 percent to the GDP of the 15 sub-Saharan Africa (SSA) countries that have relied heavily on natural resources during the past decade. In these countries, mining exports account for about 50 percent of total exports, on average. The mining sector also serves as the primary source of FDI in the region, comprising roughly one-third of total inflows in 2017, although there have been significant fluctuations over time and among individual countries due to the development and implementation of various projects. Mining activities in SSA countries are largely dominated by MNCS, as African governments and local investors frequently lack the necessary expertise to extract mineral resources. In countries that rely heavily on resource extraction, foreign-owned MNCs account for over 80 percent of entities that make payments to governments. This refers to corporate groups that operate across multiple countries (Albertin *et al.*, 2021).

Regarding the fiscal regime, the mining sector across Africa is typically regulated by a fiscal framework that incorporates royalties, corporate income tax, and, in many cases, state participation in projects through a non-controlling ownership interest, which entitles the government to dividends from the profits generated by corporations. Alternative minimum taxes (AMTs) are commonly employed to supplement corporate taxes in cases where the tax payment falls below a specific minimum threshold. However, taxes designed to target economic rents are not utilized as frequently. Furthermore, resource-intensive countries in SSA mostly rely on project-specific contracts to establish the fiscal terms applicable to mining projects, which supersede domestic revenue laws. These contracts are typically negotiated upfront and incorporate customized fiscal terms, often diverging from the commonly applicable fiscal regime. Additionally, they include provisions to stabilize the terms over time (Albertin *et al.*, 2021).

With respect to revenue performance, mining revenue in the 15 resource-intensive economies of the region averages at 2 percent of GDP, with the majority falling within the 1-3 percent range. This raises concerns that the distribution of benefits from mining activities is not equitable, with the primary beneficiaries being multinational corporations rather than the local economies and communities. This exacerbates the paradox of extensive mineral wealth coexisting with widespread poverty. Botswana stands out as an exception, with mining revenue consistently exceeding 12 percent of GDP (AU, 2010). Recent research indicates that MNE profit shifting in mining is a significant risk to revenue collection in SSA. Mining MNC tax avoidance in Africa results in an estimated annual loss of US$450-730 million in CIT revenue. Based on observed tax rate disparities between African countries and offshore MNE affiliates, the estimated loss is around US$600 million per year. Therefore, there are evident profit-shifting risks associated with corporate income tax, and these are more prevalent in the mining sector compared to other industries. Furthermore, the lack of local capacity in tax administration, policy formulation, and interagency coordination across government amplifies these risks.

The existing global tax framework could affect how producing countries tax their natural resources. Pillar I excludes natural resources from taxation as location-specific rents should be taxed in the countries where they arise. Pillar II, the global minimum effective corporate tax, could provide a new mechanism for producing countries to ensure mining MNEs pay some corporate tax and reduce tax competition (Albertin et al., 2021). However, the proposals under Pillars I and II may not tackle broader issues such as corruption and weak enforcement of regulations in Africa's extractive industries. Additionally, revenue transparency and beneficial ownership disclosure are crucial for addressing corruption and illicit financial flows in Africa's extractive industry. However, Pillar II does not directly address these issues.

4.4.2. Balancing opportunities and risks of UN resolution on tax cooperation for Africa's domestic resource mobilization

As discussed in previous sections, current international tax regulations do not adequately meet the needs of African countries. Additionally, the lack of equal, effective, and timely participation of developing countries in global governance raises concerns. Legitimate international norm-setting requires a democratic multilateral space and for this reason, the main responsibility for the issue of international tax cooperation must lie with the United Nations. Until then, Inclusive Framework members should continue demanding real and equal representation and hold the OECD accountable (Ocampo, 2018; ICRICT, 2020).

On 30 December 2022, the General Assembly adopted a resolution on the Promotion of Inclusive and Effective Tax Cooperation at the United Nations (A/

RES/77/244) (hereafter the UN resolution) which reiterates previous international pledges to increase international tax cooperation, tackle illicit financial flows, and combat aggressive tax avoidance and evasion. Subsequently, on 22 November 2023, the UN members overwhelmingly endorsed a historic resolution, led by Nigeria and the African Group, to start creating a framework convention on tax. This significant move proposes shifting global tax rule decision-making from the OECD, where it has been for over 60 years, to the UN. Despite opposition from major economies like the US, UK, and EU, the resolution passed with strong support, indicating a global consensus for more inclusive tax governance. A UK amendment to remove the convention mention was decisively rejected, with 107 countries against it and 55 for it. The final vote on the unamended resolution saw nearly two-thirds of UN countries (125) supporting the resolution, while 48 opposed and 9 abstained.

In the context of the UN resolution, international tax cooperation should promote the development of a just and efficient international tax system for sustainable development, which takes into account countries' concerns and abilities in the present and future international tax frameworks. Nonetheless, to ensure that the implementation of the resolution yields genuine benefits for Africa, it is imperative that countries efficiently navigate this complex landscape and pursue measures that support their own development objectives.

For example, there will be risks associated with the potential loss of sovereignty and the possibility that the interests of developed nations will continue to dominate the global tax agenda. There is also the risk of the potential loss of policy space and the need for African countries to balance their own interests against those of more powerful nations. It will also be critical to address information asymmetry as African countries often lack the information necessary to effectively participate in international tax cooperation. Efforts must be made to improve information exchange between countries and to ensure that African countries have access to the information they need. Addressing power imbalances head on should also be of paramount importance. African countries are often at a disadvantage in the international tax system due to power imbalances. Efforts must be made to ensure that all countries have an equal voice in the development of international tax rules at the UN. Furthermore, African countries must be supported in developing the necessary human and institutional capacity to effectively participate in the international tax cooperation process. This includes training and support for tax officials, as well as strengthening tax administrations. Additionally, efforts must continue to be made to address the root causes of illicit financial flows, including corruption and weak governance.

Other risks to consider include:

- *Limited resources*: The UN framework may lack the resources and capacity to implement its proposed measures effectively, which could limit its impact on tax collection in African countries.
- *Slow progress*: The UN framework may also be slower to develop and implement measures than the OECD/G20 Inclusive Framework on BEPS, which could delay the benefits of international tax cooperation for African countries.
- *Lack of enforcement*: The UN framework may not have the same enforcement mechanisms as the OECD/G20 Inclusive Framework on BEPS, which could limit its ability to ensure compliance with international tax standards.

In general, to ensure that African countries can propose and defend standards tailored to their specific needs within the context of the UN resolution, it is essential to provide them with sufficient flexibility and support. It also requires respecting the sovereignty of African countries and diversity of views on tax policy matters and avoiding imposing external agendas that do not align with their priorities. Engaging in meaningful dialogue with African countries to understand their specific needs and challenges can facilitate the development of tailored policies that promote inclusive and effective tax cooperation. Finally, encouraging information sharing and transparency in international tax policy discussions can enable African countries to propose and defend standards that are tailored to their specific needs.

4.4.3. The role of the African Union Commission's Tax Strategy for Africa

Regional initiatives can complement global tax reform to promote international cooperation by pursuing more ambitious cooperation where global consensus is lacking. Regional tax coordination is facilitated by similarities in economic structures, administrative capacity, and culture, making agreement potentially easier. Additionally, regional tax spillovers are often significant, raising the gains from regional coordination. Thus, there is an opportunity for regional cooperation beyond the global reform process, which can address regional profit shifting and tax competition pressures by agreeing, for example, on a regional minimum tax rate (IMF, 2023).

Box 9. Tax cooperation: A better alternative for African countries?

Attracting investments through taxation is found to be less beneficial for countries than adhering to a regional policy of harmonizing fiscal incentives, as supported by Moore and Prichard (2017). According to Edwards and Keen (1996), coordinating tax policies between countries is beneficial only if the increase in the tax base resulting from coordination is greater than the amount of tax revenue that policymakers are likely to waste or misuse. Small countries are more sensitive to capital flight, and many states are tempted to lower tax rates to attract multinational investors. Coordination of tax systems would also benefit multinationals by simplifying tax rules and removing obstacles to cross-border mergers, as noted by Sørensen (2002). In terms of coordination strategies, Bretin, Guimbert and Madiès (2002) suggest setting a minimum tax rate, while Baldwin and Krugman (2004) advocate for a rate below that adopted outside the union. The implementation of a harmonization policy should be accompanied by compensatory measures such as the regional cooperation tax (TCR) in ECOWAS, which has allowed compensation for fiscal revenue losses from intra-community exchanges, with effects varying across countries.

In this context, the African Union Commission's (AUC) Tax Strategy for Africa (hereafter the Tax Strategy), released in June 2022, may have a role to play. The AUC Tax Strategy for Africa aims to significantly improve DRM and curb illicit tax practices while promoting business growth. The EU, Finland, and Germany are co-financing the initiative, which will be led by the AUC's Department of Economic Development, Trade, Industry and Mining Development (AUC-ETIM) with technical assistance from GIZ. The Tax Strategy will prioritize international taxation, continental coordination, and DRM, with the AUC leading on tax issues and assisting member states with critical tax collection issues. Because political will is essential in driving this strategy in African countries, the AUC will lead the coordination of implementing the tax strategy, working closely with critical stakeholders, especially the Regional Economic Commissions (RECs). The Sub-Committee on Tax and IFFs Issues will drive the agenda through the Specialized Technical Committee on Finance, Monetary Affairs, Economic Planning, and Integration. The AUC-ETIM will lead the operationalization of the Tax Strategy, liaise with multiple tax stakeholders on the continent, and ensure tax policy issues are addressed at the highest political level. The overall Tax Strategy will be implemented through four pillars: (1) increasing domestic resource mobilization; (2) tackling illicit financial flows

(IFFs); (3) enhancing the effectiveness of African tax administrations; and (4) increasing Africa's voice in the global tax arena (AUC, 2022).

In the context of the UN resolution, the AUC's Tax Strategy for Africa can provide a framework for African countries to develop tax standards fit for purpose that align with the principles outlined in the UN resolution. It could facilitate greater cooperation and coordination between African nations on tax matters. This could include sharing best practices, exchanging information, and collaborating on capacity building initiatives. Another role for the Tax Strategy for Africa could be to advocate for African interests in global tax forums, such as the UN Tax Committee and the OECD. The Strategy could help ensure that African perspectives are taken into account in discussions on international tax standards and regulations, and that the voices of African countries are heard in these important fora.

4.4.4. Other regional initiatives to assist African countries in reducing tax competition through better cooperation

The African Continental Free Trade Area (AfCFTA) officially began its operational phase on 7 July 2019, during the 12th Extraordinary Session of the African Union (AU) in Niamey, Niger. The agreement had already come into effect on 30 May 2019, marking the start of an ambitious journey towards creating a single market of over 1.2 billion people and a GDP exceeding US$3 trillion, derived from 55 African countries. The AfCFTA is now the world's largest free trade agreement, surpassing even the formation of the World Trade Organization (WTO). While some countries may fear a reduction in revenue from trade taxes resulting from trade liberalization, along with concerns such as loss of sovereignty and manufacturing base, it's expected that the removal or reduction of tariffs will lead to increased imports and a broader tax base, ultimately generating more tax revenue. Additionally, the AfCFTA has the potential to drive trade creation, thus expanding the taxable base and improving people's welfare. Therefore, in the medium to long term, the AfCFTA's deeper regional integration can stimulate local production and enhance DRM in Africa (Karuhanga, 2018).

In the ECOWAS region, there is crucial need for cooperation on fiscal incentives to avoid a competitive race to the bottom and to fund infrastructure development in transport and energy. Despite fiscal incentives such as exemptions, deductions, and credits commonly used in the region, countries face challenges in creating a suitable investment climate to foster economic development. ECOWAS has introduced the Fund for the Development and Financing of the Transport and Energy Sectors (FODETE), expected to generate over US$300 million annually. The fund is to be financed through taxation on agricultural exports, hydrocarbons production, and mining levies. However, it is argued that harmonizing incentive regimes would be more beneficial than the FODETE scheme, with the success of the ECOWAS Common External Tariff (CET) Regime cited as evidence that such coordination is achievable. The proposed approach includes setting a minimum CIT at 15 percent, starting in 2023, potentially generating more revenue than the proposed 0.5 percent levy on mining exports. Such harmonization offers substantial prospects for revenue gains, particularly in the mining sector.

The Africa Co-Guarantee Platform (CGP) was established in 2018 as a transaction-based mechanism to bridge Africa's risk perception gap and enhance financing for investment and trade projects using insurance and guarantees. The platform, managed by the African Development Bank, presently has a pipeline of energy, agriculture, health, and infrastructure projects across Africa.

The CGP's six partners can assist African countries in reducing tax competition through better cooperation by providing financial guarantees and technical assistance that can help promote investment and reduce reliance on tax incentives. One such way is through providing financial guarantees to support investment and trade. By offering financial guarantees, the partners can help to reduce investment risks in African countries, enabling easier entry into the market without relying on potentially unsustainable tax incentives. Furthermore, the CGP partners can provide technical assistance to African countries, improving their investment climate through tax policy reform, capacity building for tax administration, and investment promotion. This reduces the need for tax incentives and promotes fair competition among African countries. In addition to financial and technical support, the CGP partners can advocate for improved tax policies and coordination among African countries, engaging policymakers and promoting best practices to reduce tax competition and foster fair competition. They can encourage collaboration and harmonization of tax policies to discourage harmful tax practices by multinational corporations, supporting sustainable economic growth in African countries (AfDB, 2022).

4.5. Conclusion

This chapter showed that tax collection remains a significant challenge in Africa, and there is a need to increase the tax base and ensure that everyone pays their fair share. African countries, on average, have a low tax-to-GDP ratio compared to other regions, with a significant reliance on corporate income tax from multinational corporations. However, the revenue from corporate income tax as a percentage of GDP in Africa is generally lower than in other parts of the world, highlighting the potential for improvement in tax revenue mobilization efforts. The chapter also identifies several factors contributing to the decline in corporate income tax revenue, such as poorly designed tax incentives, a large informal economy, transfer pricing practices by multinational corporations, and weak tax administration and enforcement. Therefore, an efficient taxation of multinational corporations is a crucial issue for the economic development of African countries.

The chapter also argued that African countries compete for foreign investment by offering tax incentives and exemptions, often leading to a race to the bottom where tax rates are continuously lowered. This erodes the tax base and concentrates investment in certain regions, exacerbating regional disparities. Inappropriate and wasteful tax incentives, particularly in the mining sector, are granted without proper cost-benefit analysis. Therefore, greater coordination and cooperation are needed to prevent a race to the bottom, allowing for better taxation of multinational corporations, and ensuring that foreign investment benefits all regions of the continent.

Pillars I and II of the OECD/G20 Inclusive Framework on BEPS could advance the fight against tax evasion and therefore increase resource mobilization in developed countries, but limitations exist for African countries. For example, implementation must take into account issues such as corruption and weak enforcement of regulations in extractive industries. Although revenue transparency and beneficial ownership disclosure are essential for addressing corruption and illicit financial flows, Pillar II does not directly address these issues.

Finally, to ensure African countries can benefit from the UN resolution, it's crucial to provide them with flexibility and support to propose and defend tailored tax standards. This requires respecting their sovereignty and diverse views on tax policy and avoiding imposing external agendas. The AUC's Tax Strategy for Africa can provide a framework for developing fit-for-purpose tax standards. Meaningful dialogue with African countries can facilitate the development of tailored policies that promote inclusive and effective tax cooperation. Encouraging information sharing and transparency can enable African countries to propose and defend standards that meet their specific needs in international tax policy discussions.

References

African Development Bank (AfDB) (2022) 'Africa investment forum: Harnessing guarantees and insurance to close the continental financing gap – The Africa co-guarantee platform leads the way', 27 October. Available at: https://www.afdb.org/en/news-and-events/africa-investment-forum-harnessing-guarantees-and-insurance-close-continental-financing-gap-africa-co-guarantee-platform-leads-way-55839

African Tax Administration Forum (ATAF) *2017 African tax outlook 2017*. Pretoria: ATAF. Available at: https://events.ataftax.org/index.php?page=documents&func=view&document_id=16

ATAF (2019) *The place of Africa in the shift towards global tax governance: Can the taxation of the digitalised economy be an opportunity for more inclusiveness?* Pretoria: ATAF. Available at: https://events.ataftax.org/index.php?page=documents&func=view&document_id=35

ATAF (2021a) '130 Inclusive Framework countries and jurisdictions join a new two-pillar plan to reform international taxation rules – What does this mean for Africa?', 1 July. Available at: https://www.ataftax.org/130-inclusive-framework-countries-and-jurisdictions-join-a-new-two-pillar-plan-to-reform-international-taxation-rules-what-does-this-mean-for-africa

ATAF (2021b) 'A new era of international taxation rules – What does this mean for Africa?' 8 October. Available at: https://www.ataftax.org/a-new-era-of-international-taxation-rules-what-does-this-mean-for-africa

African Union (2009) *Africa mining vision*. Addis Ababa: African Union. Available at: https://au.int/en/documents/20100212/africa-mining-vision-amv

African Union Commission (AUC) (2019) *2019 African regional integration report: Towards an integrated, prosperous and peaceful Africa*. Addis Ababa: African Union. Available at: https://au.int/sites/default/files/documents/38176-doc-african_integration_report-eng_final.pdf

AUC (2022) *Tax strategy for Africa: A future of financial independence*. Addis Ababa: African Union Commission.

Ajayi, S. and Ndikumana, L. (ed.) (2015) *Capital flight from Africa: Causes, effects, and policy issues*. Oxford: Oxford University Press.

Albertin, G. *et al.* (2021) *Tax avoidance in sub-Saharan Africa's mining sector*. Departmental paper No. 22. Washington, DC: IMF.

Ali-Nakyea, A., and Amoh, J. K. (2018) 'Have the generous tax incentives in the natural resource sector been commensurate with FDI flows? A critical analysis from an emerging economy', *International Journal of Critical Accounting*, 10(3/4), pp. 257-273.

Altshuler, R., Grubert, H. and Newlon, T. S. (1998) *Has U.S. investment abroad become more sensitive to tax rates?* Working Paper No. 6383. Cambridge, Massachusetts: National Bureau of Economic Research. Available at: https://www.nber.org/papers/w6383

Baldwin, R. and Krugman, P. (2004) 'Agglomeration, integration and tax harmonisation', *European Economic Review*, 48(1), pp. 1-23.

Belinga, V., Melou, M. K. and Nganou, J.-P. (2017) *Does oil revenue crowd out other tax revenues? Policy lessons for Uganda*. Policy Research Working Paper No. 8048. Washington, DC: World Bank. Available at: https://documents.worldbank.org/en/publication/documents-reports/documentdetail/245571493644820505/does-oil-revenue-crowd-out-other-tax-revenues-policy-lessons-for-uganda

Blomström, M., Kokko, A. and Mucchielli, J. (2003) 'The economics of foreign direct investment incentives', in Hermann, H. and Lipsey, R. (ed.) *Foreign direct investment in the real and financial sector of industrial countries*. Germany: Springer, Berlin, Heidelberg, pp. 37-60.

Bolnick, B. (2004) *Effectiveness and economic impact of tax incentives in the SADC region*. Gabarone, Botswana: SADC Tax Subcommittee, SADC Trade, Industry, Finance and Investment Directorate.

Bretin, E., Guimbert, S. and Madiès, T. (2002) 'Tax competition and the taxation of company profits: Theory and practice', *Economie & Prévision*, 156(5), pp. 15-42.

Coalition for Dialogue on Africa (CoDA) (2020) *Stemming illicit financial flows (IFFs) from Africa: The journey so far*. Addis Ababa: CoDA. Available at: https://codafrica.org/wp-content/uploads/2020/10/The-Journey-So-Far.pdf

Commission européenne (2001) *La fiscalité des entreprises dans le marché intérieur*. Rapport des services de la Commission. Brussels : Commission européenne, Direction Générale Fiscalité et Union Douanière. Available at: https://taxation-customs.ec.europa.eu/system/files/2016-09/company_tax_study_fr.pdf

Coulibaly, S. and Camara, A. (2021) *Taxation, foreign direct investment and spillover effects in the mining sector*. Working paper series No. 354. Abidjan, Côte d'Ivoire: African Development Bank.

Deblock, C. and Rioux, M. (2008) 'L'impossible coopération fiscale internationale', *Éthique publique*, 10(1).

Edwards, J. and Keen, M. (1996) 'Tax competition and Leviathan', *European Economic Review*, 40(1), pp. 113-134.

Flatters, F. (2005) *International perspectives on tax incentives in Malaysia*. Malaysian Institute of Taxation National Tax Conference 2005 "An effective tax regime, a joint responsibility", Putrajaya, Malaysia, 9-10 August. Available at: http://qed.econ.queensu.ca/faculty/flatters/writings/ff_mit_presentation.pdf

Global Alliance for Tax Justice (GATJ), Public Services International (PSI) and Tax Justice Network (TJN) (2021) *The state of tax justice 2021*. Available at: https://taxjustice.net/wp-content/uploads/2021/11/State_of_Tax_Justice_Report_2021_ENGLISH.pdf

Gubian, A., Guillaumat-Tailliet, F. and Le Cacheux, J. (1986) 'Fiscalité des entreprises et décision d'investissement. Eléments de comparaison internationale France, RFA, Etats-Unis', *Revue de l'OFCE*, (16), pp. 181-216.

Hines, J. R. (2004) *Do tax havens flourish?* NBER Working Paper No. w10936. Cambridge, Massachusetts: National Bureau of Economic Research.

Independent Commission for the Reform of International Corporate Taxation (ICRICT) (2020) 'ICRICT response to the OECD consultation on the Pillar One and Pillar Two Blueprints', 16 December. Available at: https://www.icrict.com/presse/2020-12-16-oecd-response-to-the-oecd-consultation-on-the-review-of-country-by -country-reporting-beps-action-13/

ICRICT (2022) *It is time for a global asset registry to tackle hidden wealth*. ICRICT. Available at: https://www.icrict.com/wp-content/uploads/2022/04/ICRICTGAReportEN.pdf

Institute of Development Studies (IDS) (2014) *Will changes to the international tax system benefit low-income countries?* IDS rapid response briefing No. 06. Brighton, UK: Institute of Development Studies. Available at: https://opendocs.ids.ac.uk/articles/report/Will_Changes_to_the_international_Tax_System_Benefit_Low-income_Countries_/26476909?file= 48228646

International Monetary Fund (IMF) (2023) *International corporate tax reform*. Policy paper No. 2023/001. Washington, DC: IMF. Available at: https://www.imf.org/en/Publications/Policy-Papers/Issues/2023/02/06/International -Corporate-Tax-Reform-529240

Jacquemot, P. and Raffinot, M. (2018) 'La mobilisation de ressources en Afrique', *Revue d'économie financière*, 131(3), pp. 243-263.

James, S. (2017) *Incentives and investments: Evidence and policy implications*. Washington, DC: World Bank. Available at: https://documents1.worldbank.org/curated/en/945061468326374478/pdf/588160WP0Incen10BOX353820B 01PUBLIC1.pdf

Karuhanga, J. (2018) 'Continental Free Trade Area to boost domestic tax collections – AU official', *The New Times*, 15 January. Available at: https://www.newtimes.co.rw/article/147916/News/continental-free -trade-area-to-boost-domestic-tax-collections-a-au-official

Keen, M. and Brumby, J. (2017) 'Effet d'émulation : la concurrence fiscale et les pays en développement', *Fonds Monétaires International*, 11 juillet. Available at: https://www.imf.org/external/french/np/blog/2017/071117f.htm

Kransdorff, M. (2010) 'Tax incentives and foreign direct investment in South Africa', *Consilience* (3). Available at: https://doi.org/10.7916/consilience.v0i3.4497

Mahapatra, R. (2021) 'Global corporate taxation: The new bare minimum', *ICRICT*, 2 December. Available at: https://www.icrict.com/icrict-in-thenews/2021/12/2/global-corporate-taxation-the-new-bare-minimum

McLure, C. (1986) 'Tax competition: Is what's good for the private goose also good for the public gander?' *National Tax Journal*, 39(3), pp. 341-348.

Monkam, N. F. (2011) *Building democracy in Africa through taxation*. Nairobi: Tax Justice Network – Africa.

Moore, M. and Prichard, W. (2017) *Comment les gouvernements de pays à faible revenu peuvent-ils augmenter leurs recettes fiscales ?* Document de travail ICTD 70. Available at: https://www.ictd.ac/fr/publication/comment-les-gouvernements-de-pays-a-faible-revenu-peuvent-ils-augmenter-leurs-recettes-fiscales/

Muet, P.-A. and Avouyi-Dovi, S. (1987) 'L'effet des incitations fiscales sur l'investissement', *Revue de l'OFCE*, 18(1), pp. 149-174.

Mureithi, C. (2021) 'Why Kenya and Nigeria haven't agreed to a historic global corporate tax deal?', *Quartz*, 2 November. Available at: https://qz.com/africa/2082754/why-kenya-and-nigeria-havent-agreed-to -global-corporate-tax-deal

Niang, F. (2020) 'Le rôle de la fiscalité dans le financement du développement en Afrique', *Afrique et Développement*, 45(1), pp. 133-148. Available at: https://www.jstor.org/stable/26936567

Ocampo, J. A. (2018) 'Box 0.1: The world needs to revamp international tax cooperation', in *Spotlight on sustainable development 2018*, pp. 22-25. Available at: https://www.2030spotlight.org/en/book/1730/chapter/box-world -needs-revamp-international-tax-cooperation

Organisation de coopération et de développement économiques (OCDE) (2002) *Impôt sur les sociétés et invest-issement direct étranger : L'utilisation d'incitations fiscales*. Études de politique fiscale de l'OCDE, n° 4. Paris : Éditions OCDE. Available at: https://doi.org/10.1787/9789264288409-fr

Organisation for Economic Co-operation and Development (OECD) (2017) The Yaoundé Declaration: A call for action to tackle illicit financial flows through international tax cooperation. Available at: https://www.oecd.org/tax/transparency/what-we-do/technical-assistance/Yaounde-Declaration-with-Signatories.pdf

OECD (2019) *Addressing the tax challenges of the digitalisation of the economy: Public consultation document*. OECD/G20 Base Erosion and Profit Shifting Project. Available at: https://web-archive.oecd.org/2019-02-19/507498-public-consultation-document-addressing-the-tax-challenges-of-the-digitalisation-of-the-economy.pdf

Padilla, A. *et al.* (2020) *Use and abuse of tax breaks: How tax incentives become harmful*. Washington, DC: The Financial Transparency Coalition (FTC). Available at: https://www.christianaid.org.uk/sites/default/files/2022-09/use-and-abuse-of-tax-breaks.pdf

Poitevin, M. (2018) *Concurrence fiscale et biens publics*. Montréal : Centre interuniversitaire de recherche en analyse des organisations. Available at: https://www.cirano.qc.ca/files/publications/2018RP-09.pdf

Sørensen, P. B. (2002) *The future of company taxation in the European Union*. Economic Policy Research Unit, University of Copenhagen. Available at: https://web.econ.ku.dk/pbs/diversefiler/Bolkestein.pdf

South African Institute of International Affairs (SAIIA) (2021) *Strengthening tax cooperation with Africa for sustainable revenue mobilisation*. Policy Briefings, Global Economic Governance No 256. Available at: https://saiia.org.za/research/strengthening-tax-cooperation-with-africa-for-sustainable-revenue -mobilisation/

Tax Justice Network (TJN) (2019) *Vulnerability and exposure to illicit financial flows risk in Africa*. Buckinghamshire: Tax Justice Network.

Tax Justice Network-Africa (TJN-A) (2022) *Revenue waivers and national economic pressures: The hidden cost of tax expenditures in Kenya*. Nairobi: Tax Justice Network-Africa (TJN-A), East African Tax Governance Network (EATGN) and Africa Centre for People Institutions and Society (ACEPIS).

TJN-Africa and ActionAid International (2012) *Tax competition in East Africa: A race to the bottom?* Nairobi: Tax Justice Network-Africa and ActionAid International. Available at: https://www.policyforum-tz.org/sites/default/files/2021-03/East%20Africa%20Tax%20Incentives%20Report.pdf

TJN-Africa and ActionAid International (2015) *The West African giveaway: Use & abuse of corporate tax incentives in ECOWAS*. Tax Justice Network-Africa ActionAid International. Available at: https://resourcecentre.savethechildren.net/pdf/full_report_-_the_west_african_giveaway.pdf/

United Nations (UN) and Inter-American Center of Tax Administration (CIAT) (2018) *Design and assessment of tax incentives in developing countries: Selected issues and a country experience*. New York: United Nations. Available at: https://www.un.org/esa/ffd/wp-content/uploads/2018/02/tax-incentives_eng.pdf

World Bank (2020) *Doing business report 2020: Comparing business regulation in 190 economies*. Washington, DC: World Bank Group. Available at: https://documents1.worldbank.org/curated/en/688761571934946384/pdf/Doing-Business-2020-Comparing-Business-Regulation-in-190-Economies.pdf

Zee, H. H., Stotsky, J. G. and Ley, E. (2002) 'Tax incentives for business investment: A primer for policy makers in developing countries', *World Development*, 30(9), pp. 1497-1516.

www.ingramcontent.com/pod-product-compliance
Lightning Source LLC
Chambersburg PA
CBHW080044280326
41935CB00014B/1784